values
and interests
in
social change

SISTER MARIE AUGUSTA NEAL, S.N.D.
Emmanuel College, Boston, Massachusetts

prentice-hall, inc.   englewood cliffs, new jersey

prentice-hall
contemporary problems
in sociology series

JOHN D. DONOVAN, *editor*

To My Parents

PRENTICE-HALL INTERNATIONAL, INC., *London*
PRENTICE-HALL OF AUSTRALIA, PTY., LTD., *Sydney*
PRENTICE-HALL OF CANADA, LTD., *Toronto*
PRENTICE-HALL OF INDIA (PRIVATE) LTD., *New Delhi*
PRENTICE-HALL OF JAPAN, INC., *Tokyo*

Library of Congress Catalog Card No.: 65-10181

Printed in the United States of America
93985-C   93984-P

preface

People are looking for explanations of social change today. Classic theories of Hegelian and Darwinian dimensions seem too abstract and all-inclusive to describe adequately the resistance to and acceptance of current pressures to change. Because pressures to change are at the same time part of daily experience and part of the broad historical process, it seems essential to examine the relationship between the direction of historical trends and the dialogue of decision making. One way of doing this is to analyze those factors which characterize social process at both face-to-face and mass communication levels of daily living, through a systematic study of styles of response, cliché-like expressions of conceptions of the world, characteristic ways of interacting, standards accepted, and decisions made. In this study the population sampled consisted of Catholic priests responding to current stimuli to change behaviors long-institutionalized in local community relations. These priests are currently decision-makers facing change in an historically significant moment.

This experimental study was developed in 1959 before the Second Vatican Council was announced. The dynamism of the social process is perhaps best reflected in the fact that the voices selected then to verbalize pressure to change in this study were in 1964 consultants at Vatican II. The pressures to change examined here fall into five areas of interpersonal behavior: command-obedience relations, social responsibility, independence training for children, respect for the intellectual life and motivational awareness. These are major topics under discussion at the Council.

A grant from the Ella Lyman Cabot Trust Fund allowed time and facilities for research. Special thanks are due to Richard Cardinal

iii

carry out this study and to the priests of the Boston archdiocese for their cooperation in this whole project. Thanks are due also to Father John Early, S.J., and Mrs. Dorothy Hansberry for hours of careful coding. I deeply appreciate the many discussions with and suggestions from members of the Social Relations Department at Harvard and most especially the help of Professors Arthur Couch, Robert N. Bellah, and William Gamson. Professor Talcott Parsons' ideas and suggestions were a constant stimulus through the entire period of research and writing. In the stages of thesis writing a continuing dialogue with Profesor Harry Johnson was most helpful, as were the later sessions with Professor John D. Donovan, the local editor of this series. Professor Neil Smelser's suggestions in the summer of 1963 for transforming the thesis to book form were invaluable. Finally without the constant encouragement and assistance of Sr. Miriam St. John and other members of the Emmanuel faculty and student body, this study would never have been completed. To all who helped with the extensive work entailed in the project I am deeply grateful.

Sr. Marie Augusta Neal, S.N.D.
Boston, Massachusetts

contents

v

introduction It is a pleasure to welcome Sister Marie
Augusta's study to the growing volume of high-
quality literature on social change. First
and foremost, her work has intrinsic scholarly merit. She has chosen an
important, controversial, and almost totally neglected subject for study—
the differential receptivity to cultural and social innovation within the
Catholic Church. She has approached this "hot" subject with admirable
objectivity. She has observed the canons of theoretical and methodolo-
gical discipline throughout. And she has produced a number of informed
empirical findings on the social and attitudinal bases of change in the
Church. On all these counts her work should prove a model for many
future studies.

Above and beyond its intrinsic worth, this volume stands as a symbol
of many trends—all of which I consider healthy—in the contemporary
intellectual and social world. Most important, it symbolizes the development of a trend that has become increasingly evident since World
War II—a trend emphasizing the disciplined and theoretically relevant,
but not grandiose analysis of social change. In the generation immediately preceding World War II, the systematic study of social change in
American sociology was a veritable wasteland, with the exception of
figures like Sorokin and MacIver (both non-American by origin) and, to
a lesser extent, Ogburn and Chapin. This period of indifference, even
antagonism, toward the study of large-scale institutional change resulted
from the confluence of a number of intellectual forces, among them the
defiant positivism of the 1920's and the militantly anti-evolutionary
posture of early anthropological functionalism. Only after shedding these

negativistic features was sociology able to turn again to some of the larger issues of social change. But by then sociologists were better equipped—by virtue of *not* having abandoned the preoccupation with careful empirical analysis and systematic theory bred by these very same intellectual forces—to avoid the gross errors of the late nineteenth and early twentieth centuries. In a very real sense, then, contemporary sociological interest in social change is a synthesis of the thesis of grandiosity of the generation around the turn of the century and the antithesis of theoretical timidity of the interwar period.

Sister Marie Augusta's study partakes of this synthesis. Her theoretical starting point is one of the most persistently debated sets of issues in contemporary sociological thinking: Should integrative values or conflict-producing interests be emphasized in constructing a theory of social change? Do these emphases stand in permanent contradiction, or is some synthesis possible? Instead of producing yet another polemic on these issues, however, the author has attempted to see *what difference the respective emphases make in the analysis of a particular empirical problem*, viz., how to account for the balance of forces for and against several types of change in the Church. This enterprise quite naturally forces her to define "values" and "interests" operationally with respect to the religious setting (in this case she constructed an original questionnaire to measure attitudes); to select an appropriate sample of clergymen to study; to observe the rules of careful field procedure in studying them; to quantify her results; and to bring the appropriate statistical techniques to bear on their analysis. In these senses Sister Marie Augusta's work stands out as an empirically informed *and* theoretically relevant analysis.

In general the author moves deftly to and fro among the several different levels of analysis that run through the monograph. From time to time I think her analysis is vulnerable to criticism. I suspect, for example, that the ways the concept of "interest" is used by theorists from Marx to Dahrendorf differ significantly from the way the author has represented "interest"—mainly as self-interest—in her questionnaire; this brings into question the precise theoretical bearing of the author's findings on the Marxian tradition. I sense also that sometimes the author's independent variables (the four types of orientation toward change) overlap conceptually with her dependent variables (especially the clergymen's orientations to the world as analyzed in Chapter Seven); if so, the relations between these sets of variables become correspondingly contaminated. Such problems, however, while formidable, are not altogether insurmountable with further theoretical refinement and empirical research.

The substance of the study, as well as its method of execution, is symbolic of a number of trends in American society. For too many generations now, non-Catholic Americans—both laymen and scholars—have viewed the Catholic Church as not only stubbornly resistant to change, but also as monolithically so. For many well-educated persons this view constitutes a kind of holdout amid a vast number of other, crumbling, social stereotypes. And Catholic Americans, on their side, have perhaps done less than might be expected to dispel this stereotype, since, being a minority, they have hesitated to reveal their internal diversity and conflicts publicly. In the past decade especially, a flood of changes on the international and American scene have worked to undermine this myth of the monolith. I need mention only two of the most dramatic of these changes—the striking innovations in the Church associated with the name of Pope John XXIII, and the profound modifications in American political and religious life symbolized and facilitated by the election of the late President John F. Kennedy. As regards social-science scholarship, I view the presentation of the findings in this volume as indicative of the broad onslaught against the myth. I trust that the contents of Chapters Six-Nine, which display convincingly the deep differences in both content and style of social attitudes among Catholics, will work to update many outmoded stereotypes about Catholicism and change.

Finally, the volume symbolizes a number of changes within the discipline of sociology. Sister Marie Augusta's study, while it is clearly a sociological analysis of the Catholic Church, is equally clearly neither "Catholic" nor "non-Catholic" sociology. The author has selected a theoretical apparatus, a number of variables, and a variety of research techniques on the basis of their appropriateness for analyzing a scientific problem. Her frame of reference is remarkably free, in my reading, from any moral, political, or religious presuppositions except those imposed by adherence to the scientific method. I see only good in this. Certainly one of the indicators of the progress of science—in both the natural and the social sciences—is the degree to which it has developed an autonomy *vis à vis* the "values and interests" of a particular civilization or a particular group. I welcome any new evidence—of which this book is an item—that this progress is continuing in sociology.

Neil J. Smelser

1

the function of values and interests: the theoretical problem

The on-going debate on theories of social change tends to a formulation of the problem either in a conflict frame or in a functional frame. Proponents of the two schools of thought, however, seldom reach a point of operationalizing variables and testing propositions. The main purpose of this book is to offer the experimental data found in a particular study and to work toward the development of a more comprehensive theory of social change, one suggested by Marxian and Parsonian models, but derived from empirical generalizations.

MARX AND WEBER YESTERDAY

A century ago Karl Marx asserted that social change is initiated by conflict of interest groups. He claimed that current power elites resist change in value terms. People accept responsibility to initiate change when they become aware that their special interests are in fact exploited by the very structure of the social system. The values institutionalized are in all cases the values of the ruling class. They are epiphenomena generated by the group in power to preserve the *status quo*. Marx observes in the *Manifesto*:

What else does the history of ideas prove than that intellectual production changes in character in proportion as material production is changed. The ruling ideas of each age have been the ideas of the ruling class.[1]

In statements like this one Marx takes his position with those who make a general rule of the observation that some kind of economic or other material necessity sets the direction for new social forms. Values are then generated by man in his cultural productions to legitimate the new trend in social forms.

Max Weber's explanation of the role of values in social systems stands in contrast to that of Marx. He objected to Marx's narrowed interpretation of the function of values in social systems. Without denying that values can be used as rationalizations for action chosen for interest reasons, Weber in an extended study (*The Protestant Ethic and the Spirit of Capitalism*) demonstrated the relationship between the values derived from the "Protestant Ethic" and the rise of capitalism. He showed that if, in social systems in which work is perceived as punishment for sin, this same work is presented as a calling, as a means of salvation, and a religious ideal, then the virtues of work, effort, thrift, and honesty increase among people in roles. Such virtues will then produce, as "unintended consequence," improvement of the economic system.[2] The continuation of this study, Weber's lifetime work in comparative sociology, presented evidence that the values that give legitimacy to a social system can precede in time the organizational structure of that system and hence are not necessarily epiphenomena.

Though intended as a refutation of Marx's thesis that values are generated by the interests of the power elite to reinforce their advantage, Weber's study has never been completely accepted.[3] Marx's interpretation, as well as Weber's, holds that the ideals reinforcing the

[1] Lewis S. Feuer, ed., *Basic Writings on Politics and Philosophy: Karl Marx and Freidrich Engels* (New York: Anchor Books, Doubleday & Company, Inc., 1959), p. 26.

[2] Max Weber, *The Protestant Ethic and the Spirit of Capitalism*, trans. Talcott Parsons (London: George Allen & Unwin, 1930). See also Robert Merton's "The Unanticipated Consequences of Purposive Social Action," *American Sociological Review*, I, No. 5 (1936), 894-904.

[3] See Kurt Samuelsson's *Religion and Economic Action*, trans. E. Geoffrey French (New York: Basic Books, 1961). In support of Weber see also Gerhard Lenski's *The Religious Factor* (New York: Doubleday & Company, Inc., 1961).

new economic order are created from discontent with the older order and hence are embedded in the history of that old system. But because the processes are hidden in unrecorded history of those uneventful periods between significant happenings, historical study cannot effectively demonstrate whether incipient role relations for the coming economic order precede or follow incipient evaluations of what is the "new good." It is difficult, therefore, to trace the order of emergence of values and interests in historical sequences and almost impossible to gather the data for the relation claimed by either position.[4] Sociologists since the time of Weber have tended to take sides on this issue rather than resolve it. They tend either to treat values as did Marx, that is, as important class-determined phenomena adhered to by the group profiting from them and generating them,[5] or else to treat them as part of the institutionalized culture which sets limits on choices of social forms to carry out functional needs of social systems.[6]

INTEGRATION AND CONFLICT THEORY TODAY

In proposing a structure-function theory, Talcott Parsons calls attention to a consensus which underlies conflict of interests in ongoing social systems.

In contrast to the theorists who focus on conflict of interest groups as determinants of social change, he notes the consensus underlying the conflict of interests:

It can be taken as a fundamental proposition of social science that no system of the "play of interests" can be stable unless the pursuit

[4] See Karl Marx and Freidrich Engels, *The German Ideology*, Parts I and III (New York: International Publishers, 1947), pp. 3-78, and Samuelsson, *Religion and Economic Action*.

[5] Ralf Dahrendorf is most explicit on this point as he explains that "In every association the interests of the ruling group are the values that constitute the ideology of the legitimacy of its rule, whereas the interests of the subjected group constitute a threat to this ideology and the social relations it covers." *Class and Class Conflict in Industrial Society* (Stanford, Cal.: Stanford University Press, 1959), p. 176.

[6] This kind of explanation is found in Bronislaw Malinowski, *Magic, Science, and Religion* (Boston: The Beacon Press, 1948), especially pp. 39-40; A. R. Radcliffe-Brown, *Structure and Function in Primitive Society* (London: Cohen and West, 1952); Ruth Benedict, *Patterns of Culture* (Boston: Houghton Mifflin Company, 1934), especially Chapter Two.

of these interests is carried out within an institutionalized normative system—a common framework of values, of generalized norms, and of the structuring of the interests themselves.[7]

He explains that not conflict, but the integrative function, is central to the sociologist's concern, even though he makes no claim for the level of integration in any given social system. He says in *Theories of Society*:

> For any given type of system—here, the social—the integrative function is the focus of its most distinctive properties and processes. We contend, therefore, that the problems focusing about the integrative functions of social systems constitute the central core of the concerns of sociological theory.[8]

In a statement rich in feeling and conviction about the current state of sociology, Ralf Dahrendorf underscores the fact that a divergence in view concerning the role of values in social systems and the function of conflict of interest groups is still very much alive. He observes:

> Throughout the history of Western political thought, two views of society have stood in conflict. Both these views are intended to explain what has been, and will probably continue to be, the most puzzling problem of social philosophy: how is it that human societies cohere? There is one large and distinguished school of thought according to which social order results from a general agreement of values, a *consensus omnium* or *volonte generale* which outweighs all possible or actual differences of opinion and interest. There is another equally distinguished school of thought which holds that coherence and order in society are founded on force and constraint, on the domination of some and the subjection of others. To be sure, these views are not at all points mutually exclusive. The Utopian (as we shall call those who insist on coherence by consensus) does not deny the existence of differences of interest; nor does the Rationalist (who believes in coherence by constraint and domination) ignore such agreements of value as are required for the very establishment of force. But Utopian and Rationalist alike advance claims of primacy for their respec-

---

[7] Talcott Parsons, "Polarization and the Problem of International Order," *Berkeley Journal of Sociology*, VI, No. 1 (1961), 115-34.

[8] Parsons, Edward Shils, Kaspar D. Naegele, Jesse R. Pitts, eds., *Theories of Society*, I (New York: Free Press of Glencoe, Inc., 1961), pp. 40-41.

tive standpoints. For the Utopian, differences of interest are subordinated to agreements of value, and for the Rationalist these agreements are but a thin, and as such ineffective, coating of the primary reality of differences that have to be precariously reconciled by constraint.[9]

Dahrendorf's position is typical of conflict theorist criticism of structure-function theory as presented by Parsons. It is also typical of a tendency to oversimplify the conception of social solidarity in functional theory because it assumes either mechanical solidarity or coercion, and ignores solidarity of the organic type which is central to empirical study of conflict. Another conflict theorist, C. Wright Mills, would make power the major explanatory concept for social change, and he objects to what he perceives as Parsons' value emphasis in this way:

> In the course of any substantive research, many problems do confront those who hold the view of power that I have been suggesting. But we are not at all helped by the deviant assumptions of Parsons, who merely assumes that there is, presumably in every society, such a "value hierarchy" as he imagines. Moreover, its implications systematically impede the clear formulation of significant problems. . . .
> In these terms, the idea of conflict cannot effectively be formulated. Structural antagonisms, large-scale revolts, revolutions—they cannot be imagined. In fact, it is assumed that "the system," once established, is not only stable but intrinsically harmonious; disturbances must, in his language, be "introduced into the system." The idea of the normative order set forth leads us to assume a sort of harmony of interests as the natural feature of any society; as it appears here, this idea is as much a metaphysical anchor point as was the quite similar idea among the eighteenth century philosophers of the natural order.[10]

Here Mills reads into Parsons' theoretical model of integration a claim for empirically existing perfect integration. Parsons actually makes no prejudgment of the amount of integration present in any given social system even as he emphasizes the centrality of consensus rather than conflict in social structure.

Dahrendorf would say that concern with consensus tends to focus

[9] Dahrendorf, *Class and Class Conflict*, p. 157.
[10] Mills, *Sociological Imagination* (New York: Oxford University Press, 1959), pp. 41-42.

on the normative level of social structure whereas concern with conflict tends to center attention on the behavior level. He holds that the difference in focus explains the difference in the two kinds of theory. He says:

> Parsons displays a conspicuous bias in favor of analysis in terms of values and norms. It is equally true that many of those who have been concerned with problems of conflict rather than of stability have tended to emphasize not the normative but the institutional aspects of social structure. The work of Marx is a case in point.[11]

Some integrative theorists who can explain the current controversy for themselves or who have reconciled the relationship between conflict of interests and value consensus in their own minds consider the problem solved or at least unimportant. Seymour Lipset reflected this conclusion when he reviewed Moore's *Political Power and Social Theory*. At that time he concluded: "The two kinds of explanations do not conflict but supplement one other [sic]. Amen."[12] Here he indicates his desire to consider the controversy ended. But many conflict theorists not only do not feel it is ended but also feel that the differences are in fact irreconcilable. This is evident in Mills' position on Parsonian theory just quoted from *Sociological Imagination* and in Hacker's observation:

> The "conservative" bias in Parsons' writing has been remarked upon by more than one commentator. The central place he gives to a theory of "equilibrium" in his system is made to be convincing evidence that the emphasis is on underlying social consensus rather than on continual, even irreconcilable, conflict.[13]

Though the Parsonian theorist feels this criticism "entirely misses the point," still it represents the position of the conflict school and indicates the existence of theoretical confusion.

[11] Dahrendorf, *Class and Class Conflict*, p. 160. Dahrendorf uses the word "institution" here to refer to the behavioral level where Parsons uses the same word to refer to the normative level. This adds a semantic confusion to the discussion.

[12] Seymour M. Lipset, "Political Power and Social Theory," *American Sociological Review*, XXV, No. 2 (1960), 285.

[13] Andrew Hacker in *The Social Theories of Talcott Parsons: A Critical Examination*, Max Black, ed. (Englewood Cliffs, N.J.: Prentice-Hall, Inc., 1961), pp. 290-91.

THE APPARENT DILEMMA

The examination of problems related to controversy of this type may be difficult, but one can hardly say that it is irrelevant. The theoretical literature clearly demonstrates that, although both kinds of theory treat of values and of interests, the integration theorist gives the directing role to consensus on values and the conflict theorist gives it to conflict of interests. In the integration theory, values are perceived as setting limits on the interests that can be expressed, and this is done through the sanction system; in conflict theory, interests of specific groups are perceived as generating values or manipulating existing values as a means to legitimate group-member behavior. Although no theorists ignore behaviors guided by values or interests, there is a tendency to make general statements about one of these elements being a more general determinant of the direction of change than the other.[14] The question raised here is simply—is this so? The two horns need not represent exclusive alternatives in the dilemma.[15] Values and interests could play different roles in accordance with given historical conditions. If so, the real problem is to find out what these conditions are and how they are related to differing interpretations and analyses. A study of the function of values and interests in the process of social change will not necessarily resolve the dilemma, but it should help to clarify what it is that theorists look at when they develop divergent theories to explain the same historical process. Much systematic research must be done before theoretical models can be widely accepted as descriptive of social process. The integration-conflict dilemma not only provides a stimulus for such research but it also suggests the content for research designs. The following hy-

[14] The issue involved in this discussion is not whether or not conflict and integration are opposites but rather that they are treated in the theoretical controversy as alternate explanations of the same phenomenon and this more particularly from the frame of reference of the conflict theorists when viewing the writings of functional theorists.

[15] On this same point, see Pierre L. van den Bergh's attempt at another kind of synthesis of these two positions. See his "Dialectic and Functionalism: Towards a Theoretical Synthesis," *American Sociological Review*, XXVIII, No. 5 (1963), 695-705. This article contains an extensive list of the functional thinking on this controversy.

pothetical construct, the design proposal, and the research data illustrate one kind of study possible in this relatively unexplored area.

AN OPERATIONAL PERSPECTIVE:
THE ROLE OF THE DECISION MAKER

One possible explanation of the function of values and interests in the process of social change assumes that decision makers tend to make choices either in value or interest terms. This explanation is based on the assumption of the existence of relatively stable personality characteristics. If such personality characteristics are demonstrated to be operative as determinants of the direction of choice, another set of hypotheses is required to explain why they exist and why they fulfill the function of directing choice. This double problem will constitute the first part of the study, namely (*a*) the development of a method to determine the existence of value and interest orientations as relatively permanent personality variables; and (*b*) the formulation of hypotheses to explain why they exist. The second part of the study will be an examination of their influence on the direction of social change.

Response to crisis (occasion for change) has a long history of eliciting opposite interpretations. Two ancient Chinese characters that are used to express the word "crisis" mean "danger" and "opportunity." This etymological evidence implies the presence of danger and opportunity in every crisis, but the fact remains that, even though the same world or local situation is being responded to, individual men tend to overperceive one or the other, danger or opportunity, according to more enduring characteristics of their own definitions of the world. This can be seen in responses in the field of race relations, aid to underdeveloped nations, disarmament, and ecumenism.

A dichotomous model made up of two classes of men—the change oriented and the nonchange oriented—however, would be far too simple to explain the direction of history. It would leave out the main variable found in theories of social change, the value-interest dimension. A more complete model then suggests a second division crosscutting the change and nonchange categories, characterizing orientation to choice. This can be called the value-interest dimension.

One of Talcott Parsons' pattern variable types comes close to describing this dimension, namely the particularistic-universalistic dichotomy.[16] Parsons' terms refer to the basis on which rights are claimed and obligations accepted in social systems. According to Parsons, a person universalistically oriented expects rights and accepts obligations in generalized terms independently of his particular relationship to the object, whereas a person particularistically oriented expects rights and accepts obligations in terms of the actors' particular relationship to him. One orientation emphasizes the actualization of a principle; the other shows concern for certain people. The two pattern variables, universalism and particularism, are closely related to the value and interest primacy in the Parsons-Marx theory differences. Their frequent use in analyses by sociologists indicates an awareness of the presence of such relatively enduring characteristics of men in society.

VALUE AND INTEREST ORIENTATIONS

Some discussion of the meaning of the terms "values" and "interests" is called for at this point. Values refer to widely shared conceptions of the good; societal values refer to conceptions of the good society. Interests refer to desires for special advantages for the self or for groups with which one is identified. In Neil Smelser's terms, "Interests refer to short-term desires to protect or to maximize institutionalized positions of the individual or the group." Smelser perceives a critical difference between interests and values. He maintains that "whereas we are prepared to bargain with our interests we will not enter into practical compromise with our values."[17] Presumably no one acts for change or against change unless he is interested. This is not the problem. The concern here is whether interests constitute for the actor the more dynamic criterion for choice. Is his main intention to realize an ideal or to service a group? The intention of the value-oriented actor is more to bring about in time those programs, be-

[16] The four pattern variables are treated in Talcott Parsons and Edward Shils, *Toward a General Theory of Action* (Cambridge, Mass.: Harvard University Press, 1951), pp. 76-88.

[17] These ideas of Neil Smelser's on interests and values are taken from his unpublished "Memorandum to Stouffer" circulated in Social Relation 272, a seminar on the Analysis of Social Data given in the Social Relations department at Harvard in the Spring of 1960.

haviors, and artifacts he believes reflect the values to which he is committed. The interest-oriented actor's primary intention is approval from certain people he loves, fears, respects.

Primary concern for one's own groups is a requisite of certain roles, for example, of a father's role for the protection of his family, of a businessman's for the profit of his firm, of a political leader's for the interests of his constituents. But the distinction still obtains. There are value and interest orientations for carrying out all these jobs, as evidenced in the racial integration controversy in America. In other words, though interests and values operate in everyone's choices, a very real division of belief about the legitimacy of an interest-over-value or a value-over-interest primacy colors evaluations and behavior. This primacy of one commitment over the other characterizes people in roles in many different groups irrespective of the primary functions of the group. The goals of the group do not determine the orientations of the actors, but different orientations among the actors develop the characteristic style of the group at a certain time in some complex relation to its intended goal.

Speaking then in ideal types, the value-oriented person is concerned with the achieving of a goal which is in conformity with a standard of excellence. Realization of values is his primary concern. The interest-oriented person is primarily concerned that the process of goal attainment afford advantage to certain people—to the exclusion, if necessary, of others. The value-oriented man moves from group to group ever seeking to realize the same values; the interest-oriented man moves from value to value ever seeking them for the same group.

A VALUE INTEREST—

CHANGE-NONCHANGE PARADIGM

All this discussion of values and interests, change and resistance to change, as orientations to choice constitutes an effort to construct hypothetically the definition of the situation within which man makes decisions that determine the direction of the historical process. Thus a basic assumption of this exploration is that expressed by W. I. Thomas in his famous statement: "If men define situations as real they are real in their consequences."[18] Careful observation of

[18] For a concise discussion of W. I. Thomas' well-known theorem, see Lewis A. Coser and Bernard Rosenberg, *Sociological Theory* (New York: The

decision-making situations reveals that the same situations receive quite different definitions from actors oriented to change than from actors oriented to resist change. The heroes and villains are different and the approved policies differ. Further observation reveals another breakdown within the change and nonchange groups: justifications of decisions in terms of interest or in terms of value. Thus, in any given situation facing change, four types of responses can be distinguished among the actors, depending on their definitions of the situation: a value-change orientation, an interest-change orientation, a value-non-change, and an interest-nonchange orientation. (Henceforth, these four orientations will sometimes be referred to by the abbreviations VC, IC, VNC, and INC.) Instead of determining the existence of just value and interest orientations, the model for the study has now been expanded to four categories: VC, IC, VNC, and INC. The first research task is the development of a measuring instrument that will determine the evidence for the existence of these four types of orientation to action in decision-making situations.

ORIENTATION AND THE FUNCTIONAL PROBLEMS

The following discussion introduces some speculations as to why these four orientations might be expected to be present as relatively enduring personality characteristics in any choice-making situation. Parsons' fourfold table of functional requisites presents a basis for speculation about the existence of such orientation.[19]

The functional problems of adaptation, integration, goal attainment, and pattern maintenance, according to Parsons' formulation, require for their fulfillment that different individuals in society be more or less committed to them. The essential function in *pattern maintenance* is "maintenance, at the cultural level, of the stability of institutionalized values through the processes which articulate values with the belief system, namely, religious beliefs, ideology, and the like."[20] *Goal attainment* entails "motivation to contribute what is necessary for the functioning of the system; these 'contributions' vary

---

Macmillan Company, 1957), pp. 207-11. Parsons has clarified that ideology is equivalent to definition of the situation in *Berkeley Journal of Sociology*, VI, No. 1 (1961), 115-34.

[19] Parsons *et al.*, *Theories of Society*, pp. 38-41.
[20] *Ibid.*, p. 38.

according to particular exigencies. . . . A goal is therefore defined in terms of equilibrium. It is a directional change that tends to reduce the discrepancy between the needs of the system, with respect to input-output interchange, and the conditions in the environing systems that bear upon the 'fulfillment' of such needs."[21] The *adaptive function,* according to Parsons, refers to the problem of costs. It has to do with the determination of use of facilities when several alternate goals have overlapping needs of them.[22] *Integration* is the mutual adjustment of units of social systems whether these be persons in roles or subsystems "from the point of view of their 'contributions' to the effective functioning of the system as a whole."[23]

These are the four functional areas as Parsons has defined them in his analysis of social systems in general. If we remain within the limits these functions demand, the model construction problem is to relate them to the VC, IC, VNC, and INC orientations discussed earlier. The object is not to fit new concepts to a formal model but to find out if any of these four orientations (VC, IC, VNC, INC) provides a better solution for certain functional problems. If so, then, personalities conditioned in one of these directions might tend to perceive the whole social system with a bias in the direction of the functional problem most congenial to their predispositions. This problem could be phrased just as validly by asking: Does experience with one functional problem in a social system predispose one to a VC, IC, VNC, or INC orientation in other choice-making situations? Questions related to the functional categories provide a rich source of hypotheses about expected behaviors in response to stimuli to change, and, if relationships are found, act further as an empirical test of the validity of the theoretical framework.

Specialization within the field of social relations provides examples of frames of reference that give primacy to one functional problem rather than another. A cultural anthropologist, for example, tends to observe society from the pattern maintenance frame of reference. Meanings and their symbolic and logical analysis are his primary concern. Defining these meanings, explaining, analyzing, and exploring

[21] *Ibid.,* p. 39.
[22] *Ibid.,* p. 40.
[23] *Ibid.*

them are his preoccupation. He describes social systems in terms of the network of meanings and symbols that characterize and make unique existing sociocultural configurations.[24] The political sociologist, on the other hand, tends to perceive society from the point of view of the goal-attainment function. His perception of the system focuses on the command-obedience relations which operate to achieve already defined goals. His focus is not on meanings but on people in roles, cooperating, competing, and conflicting as they strive to achieve their goals and the goals of the social system. The function of power, its legitimation in authority, and people's manipulation of the meaning system to promote goal attainment form his object of analysis.[25] The personality theorist, concerned with the process by which the unsocialized individual comes to reflect the norms of the social system, concentrates sociologically on the integration function. His problem is to study how the sanctions operate to channel undifferentiated energy in the form of gross affection and aggression tendencies into expected patterns of behavior for carrying out role behavior pre-specified by system norms. Individual deviancy, pathologies, the social-ization process insofar as it handles the process of learning in its affective forms rather than its content (a pattern maintenance prob-lem) are objects of his analysis.[26] The specialist in social change is primarily concerned with adaptation. Functional problems relating to all areas of input are generated by human capacities and potentialities, as well as by physical, psychological, social, and cultural limitations and opportunities. These problems become the object of his examina-tion because they require adaptations oriented away from what is currently institutionalized for handling pressing problems.[27]

To test the validity of these speculations, it is now necessary to ground them in a systematic study of some historically actual situa-tion currently facing change. This will indicate whether the VC, IC,

---

[24] A classic example of this orientation is Benedict's *Patterns of Culture*.

[25] C. Wright Mills in *The Power Elite* (New York: Oxford University Press, 1956) reflects this position. See also Dahrendorf, *Class and Class Conflict*.

[26] Eric H. Erickson, *Childhood and Society* (New York: W. W. Norton & Company, Inc., 1950).

[27] Unlike the other three areas no professional style has yet developed in the examination of social change. This fact reflects the confusion of theory in this field.

VNC, and INC categories are really present in a sample of the population and whether role types related to the functional categories are reflected in responses to change-oriented stimuli.

THE TEST MODEL:
FOUR TYPES OF RELIGIOUS ROLES

The problem chosen for examination deals with current changes in the Church. The sample under examination was selected from the clergy of the Catholic archdiocese of Boston as they interact in the local community. This population was chosen because there is evidence in current literature that it is being pressured to change role behavior long institutionalized but currently evaluated as dysfunctional in the face of modern exigencies. Evidence for this proposition will be presented in detail in Chapter Two.

To clarify what is meant by a relation between functional specialization and attitude toward social change, Table 1.1 describes members of the clergy oriented to the four functional areas. Later in this study an analysis of interview protocols will investigate whether or not these orientations to functional specialization really exist and whether they are related significantly to attitudes toward change, values, and interests.

According to this model, four types of religious roles ought to be distinguishable in a religious system. The first is the prophet committed to the basic values of Christianity. He adheres to the specific system in its present form only to the degree that its institutions and behavior express certain fundamental themes. Whenever the existing system does not express what he believes is the way man is to achieve his ultimate destiny, he urges change at all levels: roles, norms, goals, and values. He belongs to the system only because he shares its purpose of relating man to God according to Gospel directives. He influences the system if he can demonstrate that his message is from God and thus supersedes any traditional norm. All religions have had characteristically two sets of people in roles with reference to the message or the Word—the priest who preserves the long tradition and the prophet who shows the new way.[28]

[28] See François Mauriac, "Traditionalists and Innovators: Foes within the Church?" *Cross Currents*, XII, No. 1 (1962), 1-11, and Christopher Dawson,

table 1.1

PREDICTED ROLE PATTERNS OF CLERGY HAVING A VALUE-CHANGE, VALUE-NON-CHANGE, INTEREST-CHANGE, INTEREST-NONCHANGE ORIENTATION TO THE SOCIAL SYSTEM

—————————————— *Change Oriented* ——————————————

Value Oriented The Prophet (A)	*Interest Oriented* The Cosmopolitan Organizational Man (G)
Individuals primarily oriented to the function of adaptation will identify with the ultimate values of Christianity but will have no deep binding commitment to any specific goals or norms defined and structured through time, especially if they seem no longer functional for the expression to the world of these ultimate values. Their major concern is articulation of the system with the larger community. They are more aware of the current needs of the world at large and the areas in which institutionalized patterns in the Church are not satisfying those needs. Their identification with the values is their major source of acceptance within the system; their orientation to change makes them more acceptable to members of the larger community who feel alienated from the Church in her historic role. Their emphasis is on the articulation of the system with society at large.	Individuals primarily oriented to the attainment of the specific goals defined in time by the Church's functionaries belong here. Their deep binding commitment is primarily to the goals which they strive to attain by traditional or change-oriented methods, whichever seem to promise the most effective realization of goals. Their ego involvement is identified with the interests of the Church with respect to its current goals. Even ultimate values at times are made subsidiary to the attainment of these goals. The action of the role players may at times appear arbitrary, power oriented, and non-normative. Their emphasis on organization and power to achieve their ends is cause of concern for externs, a security for the dependent, and a worry at times to the value-oriented members of the Church.

Religion and Culture (New York: Meridian Books, 1958). Here Dawson describes the priest as "charged with the function of maintaining relations between the society and the divine powers" (p. 50), and the prophet as an agent of change claiming special authority by way of vision and inspiration (pp. 81-84). This he describes as defining the "double role religion plays in relation to culture: (a) as a unifying force in the creation of a cultural synthesis and (b) as a revolutionary disruptive force in times of social change" (p. 202).

table 1.1 continued

──────────────────────── Nonchange Oriented ────────────────────────

Value Oriented (L) The Priest	Interest Oriented The Local Organizational Man (I)
Individuals oriented to latent pattern maintenance are primarily identified with the values traditionally stressed in the system. It is their concern to preserve whatever patterns have implemented the expression of these values in time. The fact that in the course of time the former implementation might have become less effective is rather difficult for them to perceive since their major experience is concentrated within the system. Deviations from expectation are defined as failure to follow the pattern on the part of individuals, rather than as failure of effectiveness of the system itself. This is very much reinforced through their consideration of the fact of God Himself acting through the system in time. Emphasis is on articulation of the system with God. They see norms and goals as inspired by God to inculcate values; hence, though they would never sacrifice a value in order to preserve either of these structures, they are not oriented to criticism of these aspects of the system, assuming they operate with God's approval.	Individuals primarily oriented to the integrative functions of the Church tend to stress the primacy of the normative system. Ritual regularity is the major concern. Both goals and values can be made subservient to procedure. Any deviation from the traditional normative pattern appears to them as a threat to the integrity of the total system. The mere suggestion of change in any aspect of the Church's structure is defined as heresy and tremendous affect can be released at the very suggestion of change. Their ego involvement is deeply imbedded in the normative structure. Their behavior is the target of much criticism currently. Role players with this primacy can be so identified with the norms that both goals and values are sacrificed to means. The ritual and the symbols come to be perceived as effective in their own right. The effective implementation of values is sacrificed in the interest of preserving the current pattern.

Both are committed to ultimate values but the priest is committed to them only in their institutionalized form. For him the system is blessed because God acts in it. The priest and the prophet have ever been at odds. It is probable that correlates of the priest and prophet roles can be found in any social system.

If the priest and the prophet are primarily oriented to God, there are in the Church, as in all other social systems, other roles fundamentally oriented to the preservation and development of the organization itself. Perhaps the word "church-functionary" is appropriate for the goal-oriented and the integration-oriented, and refers to those more intent on carrying out a program than on examining, evaluating, or initiating it. On the one hand, there are those functionaries oriented to the control of the system and, on the other hand, those whose concern is to preserve and reinforce the whole normative structure. These latter are people that Durkheim describes, whose religious function is to reinforce social solidarity through ritual and song.[29]

All priests in the Church are empowered to perform all the functions related to preaching, teaching, administering the sacraments, carrying out the ritual that embodies the doctrine, regulating, directing, and leading in all the activities perceived as the work of the Church. But in reality there is a tendency for individuals to emphasize different areas.

This model, as well as the functional assumption on which it is based, suggests that individuals tend to specialize in the performance of some functions, and the system changes direction through time as these functional specialists interact with each other, and, through their decisions, determine the style of the system. Cooperation, competition, and conflict are involved and these in degrees and ways that in any given system can be measured. From these measures the direction of change is determinable to some degree. This, in any event, is what the following research proposes to demonstrate.

SUMMARY

It has been proposed that social change will be better understood as a social process when we know more about the ways values and interests are used as choice determiners by people facing change in the historical situation in which they play significant parts. The central hypothesis proposes that the way role incumbents respond to pressures to change that which is currently institutionalized in the community is characterized by an orientation to change or non-

[29] Emile Durkheim, *Elementary Forms of Religious Life*, trans. Joseph W. Swain (London: George Allen & Unwin, 1915), pp. 202-28 and especially p. 225.

change and to values or interests as determinants of choices in social situations. It is further hypothesized that these orientations to change and nonchange, values and interests, reflected in liberal and conservative attitudes and in universalistic and particularistic orientations to action, derive from, or at least are significantly related to, a primacy of concern for one or another of four system problems: adaptation, goal attainment, integration, and pattern maintenance. It is expected that examination of the responses made by a sample of people in roles facing real, historically grounded pressures to change will reveal this primacy of concern for certain system problems. It is further expected that their responses will reveal consistent types of resistance to and acceptance of change that will characterize their views of the world, their ways of agreeing and disagreeing, the defenses they use, and the very verbal style of their responses. Examination of these characteristic responses will indicate how value and interest orientations function in the process of social change. With this evidence it should then be possible to make some statements about the part that ideas concerning conflict of interest groups and value orientations of social groups should play in theories of social change, so that these theories will explain the actual social process and be useful for predicting the direction that social change may be expected to take in the future.

2

doctrinal and historical bases of pressures to change

Any social system manifestly facing current pressures to change could be used as the object for analysis of the functions of values and interests in the process of social change. The Catholic Church as it currently operates in local parishes and through diocesan offices presents at the present moment a particularly pertinent object for such an analysis. Increasingly since World War II, five areas of interpersonal relations within the Church have been objects of critical reevaluation which is currently generating genuine and urgent pressures to change. The areas include command-obedience relations, social responsibility, independence training for children, respect for the intellectual life, and motivational awareness.

The conditions calling for change began to be evident in the Church in the nineteenth century, and men like Archbishop Ireland of St. Paul, Minnesota, became symbols of reform especially on the continent.[1] Early efforts met resistance, and fear of heresy characterized response. The careful theological work of defining the problems in value terms was done predominantly in France.[2] American Catholic thought was

---

[1] See Thomas T. McAvoy, C.S.C., *The American Heresy in Roman Catholicism, 1895-1900* (Notre Dame, Ind.: University of Notre Dame Press, 1963).

[2] James Connolly, in *The Voices of France, A Survey of Contemporary Theology in France* (New York: The Macmillan Company, 1961), discusses why

19

sensitized to these central problems through the translations of such works as Cardinal Suhard's *Growth or Decline*,[3] and Yves Congar's penetrating theological study of clergy-laity relations in the area of obedience and independence training.[4] Today theologians, social scientists, philosophers, and innumerable others within the Church have so exerted pressures to change that local Churchmen have to face these pressures or else develop mechanisms to resist, ignore, or escape them. Criticisms from within the Church are currently converging with familiar pressures for change from outside the Church.[5]

A long history of certain styles of behavior related to the five strain areas has come to characterize communities that are predominantly Catholic. Grounded in certain doctrinal emphases as well as in response to situational stimuli, legitimation of these behaviors can be traced through historical records. In order to ground the current stimuli to their sources it will be necessary now to review these historical roots.

THE DOCTRINAL BASE:
THE TWO GREAT COMMANDMENTS

The strains in any social system arise from its purpose as specified in its goals, its standards for performing its tasks, and the nature of the tasks themselves. A religious system has for its primary

---

France has been the center of theological creativity and how the works of several of the authors used in this study were received by conservative elements in the Church.

[3] Emmanuel Cardinal Suhard, *Growth or Decline? The Church Today,* trans. James Corbett (South Bend, Ind.: Fides Publishers, 1948).

[4] Yves Congar, *Lay People in the Church,* trans. D. Attwater (Westminster, Md.: Newman Press, 1957).

[5] The entire issue of *Cross Currents*, XII, No. 2 (1962) is devoted to pressures to change written by Catholic, Anglican, Orthodox, and Protestant contributors, each indicating from his frame of reference what he sees as needed reform in the Church. Books like Ignazio Silone's *Bread and Wine,* trans. Harvey Fergusson (New York: Atheneum Publishers, 1962), express the position of the disillusioned Socialist who found the Church not living the gospel. The nineteenth century works of Dostoevsky and Nietzsche express the deep roots of these pressures in world views, and the current popularity of existential phenomenology, neo-Positivism, Marxism, and psychoanalytic theory indicates the kinds of change that resistance to such pressures tends to generate.

purpose the relating of man to the transcendent.[6] It expresses man's dependence on God manifested usually in carrying out a directive given in revelation. The central directive of the Judaic-Christian revelation is expressed in two great commandments: "Thou shalt love the Lord thy God with thy whole heart, with thy whole soul, with thy whole strength, and with thy whole mind," and "Thou shalt love thy neighbor as thyself."[7]

HISTORICAL EMPHASIS ON TRANSCENDENCE AND IMMANENCE

From these directives follow the problems that have marked the history of the Church through time, problems which have grown out of the transcendence-immanence dilemma set up by the command to love both God and man. The dilemma is always present: shall the emphasis be on God or on man? on withdrawal from the world or engagement in it? History is full of evidence of overcommitments in both directions, the one overemphasizing the action of God in the world; the other the action of man.[8] Theological positions have developed to define both emphases as good, and heresies have been condemned because of overemphasis in both directions. Within the last century both extremes have manifested themselves and been condemned, the one as Jansenism, the other as Modernism. Cardinal Suhard's description of these heresies clarifies some of the factors involved. Of the errors in the transcendent direction, he says:

This is the error of a certain group of Christians whom we may call Quietists or Jansenists depending on whether they emphasize the uselessness of the world or its harmfulness. The Quietists say that life in this world matters little as regards the eternal life. Hence, why should the Church bother about this world? Action is useless. God sees to it that the Church endures. Structures and adaptations ought to give way to confidence in God and in prayer: the supernatural can get along without natural means. So does the Church. . . . The world and Christianity are

---

[6] Christopher Dawson, *Religion and Culture* (New York: Meridian Books, 1958), pp. 25-44.

[7] Matthew 22:34-41; Deuteronomy 6:5; Leviticus 19:18.

[8] See Pierre-Augustin Leonard, "The Christian and the Non-Christian," *Cross Currents*, VIII, No. 1 (1958), 9-18 and Thomas Merton, "Christianity and Mass Movements," *Cross Currents*, IX, No. 3 (1959), 201-11.

two different systems which require a divorce, not a reconciliation. The duty of believers is not to influence events, but to be simply true disciples of Christ in their private life.[9]

On the error of immanence Cardinal Suhard comments:

Fifty years ago, overwhelmed by the conquests of modern thought, certain Catholics, insufficiently aware of the transcendent value of their faith, attempted an adaptation which amounted to an abandonment of doctrine. What mattered, they thought, was to reconcile themselves with the world. If therefore some concessions were necessary to harmonize dogma with reason, or ethics with science, we must consent to them. Everything evolves in the world. . . . If the Church wants to live, let her adapt her dogma, her worship and her discipline to the needs of the present.[10]

The voices of those pressuring for change today agree that the times call for immanent action. The great issue of our day is transcendence-immanence. According to Daniélou: "Today the Christian's first duty is to rediscover the meaning of God and bring Him to our age."[11] "Political or social engagement is, for the Christian today, an answer to a divine call,"[12] and "modern man knows that his greatest responsibility consists in improving institutions," for "in the depths of his conscience he knows that he will have to give the Sovereign Judge an account not only of his personal conduct but of the efforts he has made to solve the wage and housing problems, and to promote world peace. He knows that a few private acts of charity will be no dispensation."[13]

This immanent emphasis is expressed with genuine assurance by Father Daniélou in 1960, yet, all five of the problem areas pressuring for change originate in a long history of transcendent emphasis that has resulted in relative neglect of immanent concerns. Several studies appearing in the last ten years trace the historical groundings of the problems to a few transcendent choices that have marked the history

[9] Suhard, *Growth or Decline?*, pp. 54-55.
[10] *Ibid.*, pp. 45-46.
[11] Jean Daniélou, S. J., *The Christian Today*, trans. Kathryn Sullivan (New York: Desclee, 1960), p. 10.
[12] *Ibid.*, p. 50.
[13] *Ibid.*, pp. 121-22.

of the Church since the thirteenth century.[14] These transcendent-oriented choices fall into three areas: (1) an emphasis on monastic spirituality to the neglect of a special spirituality for the laity living in the world;[15] (2) an emphasis on that aspect of the Church which defines it as a sacramental system facing God and a concomitant de-emphasis on the Church as a community of the faithful;[16] (3) an emphasis on individual perfection and the salvation of one's own soul to the neglect of a spirituality of the "Mystical Body" and of the transformation of the world in Christ.[17] These three areas of trans-cendent emphasis require detailed consideration.

Monastic Spirituality: A Transcendent Emphasis

The emphasis on a monastic spirituality can be traced back to the early days of the Church. It refers to a preference for the religious experience of the monk characterized by the taking of the three vows of poverty, chastity, and obedience, and the living apart from the world and its political, economic, and secular concerns. The glorification of this form of life as the ideal for the Catholic has generated ambiguity concerning spirituality for the laity, whose choice

[14] See for example: Congar, *Lay People in the Church*; William Ferree, S. M., *The Act of Social Justice* (Dayton, O.: Marianist Publications, 1951); Thomas E. O'Dea, *American Catholic Dilemma: An Inquiry into the Intellectual Life* (New York: Sheed & Ward, 1958); Hans Küng, *The Council, Reform and Reunion* (New York: Sheed & Ward, 1961); Ernan McMullin, "Science and the Catholic Tradition," *America*, December 12, 1959, pp. 346-50; John Tracy Ellis, "American Catholics and the Intellectual Life," *Thought*, XXX, No. 3 (1955), 351-88; Gustave Weigel, S.J., "American Catholic Intellectualism—A Theo-logian's Reflections," *Review of Politics*, XIX, No. 3 (1957), 275-307; Karl Stern, *The Third Revolution* (New York: Harcourt, Brace & World, Inc., 1954).

[15] Augustine Cardinal Bea, "The Council and Christian Unity," *Cross Currents*, XII, No. 2 (1962), 255-68.

[16] Congar, *Lay People in the Church*. Although the ideas presented in this chapter can be documented from several sources, the work of Congar, and especially his book cited in the note, has been the major reference.

[17] Ferree's *The Act of Social Justice* is an exhaustive study of this problem. It is an analysis of the Thomistic concept of legal justice, with special reference to the doctrine of social justice emphasized by Pope Pius XI in two encyclicals, *Quadragesimo Anno* and *Divini Redemptoris*. Its purpose is to deter-mine the precise nature of the act of the virtue of social justice. Since it is Father Ferree's intention to demonstrate that this determination was not made clear before the 1930's, his study covers the major works in moral theology used in the Church in the past six centuries.

of life in the world makes them, with reference to this ideal, only second-class Catholics.[18] It is only today that this condition is being confronted as a serious problem for the Church in the realm of social responsibility and respect for the intellectual life.[19] In his extensive study of the laity in the Church, for example, Yves Congar has pointed out that it is only now in the twentieth century that the Church has developed a genuine and pervasive awareness of the need of a distinctly lay spirituality, that is, of a form of holiness suited particularly to life in the world characterized by active participation in political, economic, and social roles. "It does not appear from the apostolical writings," he observes, "that Christians interested themselves in the progress of the world they lived in. . . . With regard to society, the recommended attitude was one of respect and conformity modified by a certain indifference to things."[20] This attitude, he explains, was a result of the early Christians' believing that the world would soon end; hence they did not concern themselves with it.

St. Augustine's *City of God* reinforced this ordering of all things to one's last end, and not until St. Thomas Aquinas wrote did Christians have an authoritative statement on the goodness of valuing things for their own sake.[21] But even though St. Thomas' analysis of the good in things gave legitimacy to the Renaissance, the scientific and technological revolutions, and all the humanist developments from that time to this, this concern for things of this world still remained problematic. Most spiritual writings all through the era from the thirteenth to the twentieth century manifest this ambiguity particularly because of two historical incidents that tended to place suspicion on the intention of the laity acting on its own initiative. The first of these was the upsurge of simony and nepotism that marked the era of lay investiture prior to the reform of Gregory VII (1073-1085). The second historical issue reinforcing the monastic preference was the

---

[18] Congar, *Lay People in the Church*, pp. 1-2 and John D. Gerken, S.J., *Toward a Theology of the Layman* (New York: Herder and Herder, 1963).

[19] See Schema of Vatican Council II on the Laity, November, 1963 and October, 1964. When this study was developed, Vatican Council II had not yet been proposed, yet its content confirms the urgencies expressed in the pressures to change.

[20] 1 Peter 4:7; Congar, *Lay People in the Church*, pp. 381 and 382.

[21] *Ibid.*, p. 391.

Protestant Reformation, which specifically initiated a program of lay spirituality outside the Catholic Church. The experience with lay control in the Church prior to the thirteenth century had initiated a jealous clerical control of all Church activities and the resulting extreme clericalism later initiated the Protestant revolt. This in turn reinforced the clerical emphasis within the Church in the post-Reformation reforms and even introduced a sort of semimonastic life for the diocesan clergy.[22]

The Church as a Sacramental System Facing God: A Transcendent Emphasis

The second transcendent emphasis shaping the history of the Church and forming part of the background of the current pressures to change is the selective stress on the Church as a hierarchical, sacramental system facing God. This is a contrast to its other function as a community of the faithful.

This problem is basic to Protestant-Catholic differences on the concept of what the Church is. Before the fourteenth century the two concepts of the Church as (*a*) a community of the faithful and (*b*) an institutional means of salvation were highly integrated. From the end of the thirteenth century in the Church, one can trace an increasing emphasis on the Church as a hierarchical system for the control and distribution of the means of salvation including dogma, sacraments, and apostolic ministries. Incipient in the "apostolic" sects of the thirteenth century is a counter trend toward the communal aspect of the Church. By the sixteenth century the dominant tendency to stress the hierarchical power of the Church and hence to enhance the status of the clergy was so institutionalized that those opposed to this trend, the Protestant reformers, chose to leave the traditional Church and to establish churches which emphasized the communal aspect. At this time *De Ecclesia*, formal treatises defining the Church, were written and promulgated. Under the influence of the revival of

---

[22] Congar, *Lay People in the Church*, pp. 382-92. Hegel made similar observations in the early nineteenth century when he spoke of the Middle Ages as characterized by separation of the spiritual from the secular principle by the monastic vows of poverty, chastity, and obedience. George Wilhelm Friedrich Hegel, *The Philosophy of History*, trans. J. Sibree (New York: Dover Publications, Inc., 1956), pp. 380-81.

Roman law, which claimed absolute power of the ruler over a given territory and did not consider corporate unity, the Church as a hierarchical sacramental system facing God was formally defined as the total image of the Church.[23] This definition was reinforced by the fact that the Protestants were then emphasizing the Church as a community of the faithful. Thus, the pattern was set for the future course within the Church away from stress on the communal aspect, which was defensively perceived then as Protestant and hence negatively valued, toward the stress on hierarchy and the organization of the priesthood. From the fifteenth century, Protestants and Catholics have de-emphasized one or the other of these traditional concepts of the Church. The effects of this selective emphasis are reflected in the subsequent theologies of the two Churches and the current ecumenical movement. At the present time, there is evidence of a reversal of concern as the Protestant churches are developing a more sacramental service, while the Catholic ecumenical concern is with the Church's engagement in the community and the role of the laity in the Church.[24]

Current critics suggest that the Church today is facing an entirely new functional exigency with respect to clergy-laity relations and that the situation calls for new definitions in order to fulfill the fundamental purposes of the Church. None of them perceive the current institutionalization as requisite to Church survival. It is this openness to structural changes in the sociological sense that tends to differentiate the contemporary prophet of immanence from the institutionally committed. The problems of command-obedience relations and independence training become manifest in the Church as a result of the hierarchical emphasis.

[23] Congar, *Lay People in the Church*, pp. 22-52. The treatises on the Church promulgated in the Counter Reformation era and discussed here by Congar can now be compared with the new treatise on the Church under discussion at Vatican Council II in October and November of 1963 and October 1964, wherein the focus is on the Church as "the people of God" and not on the Church as a hierarchical institution. To see the lively discussion of difference among the council delegates on this issue in the first session of Vatican II, see Xavier Rynne, *Letters from Vatican City* (New York: Farrar, Straus & Company, 1963), pp. 214-39.

[24] Robert McAffee Brown and Gustave Weigel, *An American Dialogue* (New York: Doubleday & Company, Inc., 1960).

Individual Perfection: A Transcendent Emphasis

The third transcendent emphasis characteristic of the historical development of the Church is an individuality which has only recently been challenged by doctrinal emphasis on the "Mystical Body" theme. This individual emphasis, found also in Protestant spirituality, focuses on a personal type of religious experience in which the individual considers himself and God to the relative exclusion of his neighbor and the obligation of loving service to him. This is what Father Nevins has called the "Jesus and I" concept of religion.[25] This mode of religious instruction and practice considers the soul and God alone in the working out of one's salvation. It tends to define service to the neighbor as "works of supererogation," that is, as recommended but not required for personal sanctification.[26] Until the new concern with the doctrine of the Mystical Body developed in the twentieth century, the bulk of spiritual reading recommended to Catholics for two centuries emphasized this private spirituality. Abbé Michonneau sees it as one of the main reasons why some trained Catholics lack zeal for the social apostolate.[27] Problems centering around need for motivational awareness also derive from this emphasis.

[25] Albert S. Nevins, "Personalism Stifling Apostolic Spirit," *World Campus*, November 1960, p. 1.

[26] This emphasis was expressed by L. C. McHugh, S.J., in "Ethics at the Shelter Door," *America*, September 30, 1961, p. 825, wherein he makes normative the minimum man must do to keep out of hell rather than what constitutes the Christian way of life. In this way, the Christian concept of charity becomes itself a work of supererogation. Fr. McHugh says: "To say that one has the right to employ violence in defense of life is not to say that one has the duty to do so. Indeed, in the Christian view, there is a great merit in turning the other cheek and bearing evil patiently out of love of God. But it should be noted that people who consistently manifest this *exalted brand of supernatural motivation* [italics mine] are deservedly called heroic Christians. Their conduct reveals a dedication to the full Christian ethic that is far above what God requires *under pain of eternal loss* [italics mine] in the way of the Ten Commandments. Nowhere in traditional Catholic morality does one read that Christ, in counseling non-resistance to evil, rescinded the right of self-defense which is granted by nature and recognized in the legal system of all nations." See on this point W. K. Grossouw, *Spirituality of the New Testament* (St. Louis, Mo.: B. Herder Book Company, 1961), especially Chapter Four, "The Two Commandments," pp. 47-60.

[27] Abbé Michonneau, *Revolution in a City Parish* (Westminster, Md.: Newman Press, 1949).

Historically within the Church these emphases set the religiously valued style of life in one direction only: the direction of transcendence, of withdrawal from the world, of quiet contemplation alone with God. In gospel language, this means that the role of Mary took so much precedence over that of Martha that special *apologiae* had to be written to defend the legitimacy of social reform, and even these apologies denied the value of people and things for their own sake. Other historical factors are now resulting in a new interest in the long-neglected immanent focus with special emphasis on social relations for the development of social reforms.

Rising Interest in Clergy-Laity Relations: An Immanent Emphasis

From the end of the thirteenth century and while the Church was pursuing the transcendent emphasis, more or less withdrawn from active participation in the shaping of the world as a here-and-now entity, the impact of new social forces caused a restructuring of the secular social order and the Church's place in it. These forces included the development of a this-worldly oriented art, literature, and philosophy categorized today as the humanism of the Renaissance, which in turn fostered the emergence of the scientific method as a pre-eminent tool for intellectual inquiry about all forms of order in the universe. From these forces also developed the technological discoveries that became in time the industrial revolution. Then followed the political and social adjustments that produced urban society and democratic forms of government. Subsequently a more universal demand for training and education expanded opportunities for economic upgrading and hastened the breakdown of rigid class lines common to earlier agricultural societies of the peasant-elite type.[28]

In a new open-class system, the population had "become of age" and the father-child, mother-child, as well as the sibling models, be-

---

[28] McMullin, *America*, December 12, 1959, p. 347. "During the time when the 'modern' mind was being molded by intellectual giants like Newton, Leibnitz and Kant, the Church was voiceless and intellectually almost impotent; she could take no part in directing the flood of new ideas. The age of Newman and Mercier, and Lemaitre was still a long way off." This entire article is informative.

came restricted to the family. These were no longer legitimate sets of norms for defining the right way to act in other social systems. This does not mean that the present population of societies around the world is mature. The analysis simply indicates that, in the process of structural differentiation[29] which has been going on in Western society since the beginning of the Christian era, the family is no longer a universally functionally effective model. The economy, the polity, and other social systems have goals which necessitate more peer-like relations in the interdependencies that have developed with the specialization of function. These systems also require greater resiliency in moving from the leader to the follower role than is possible in a system that particularizes the leader role in a stable family model. Within the Church, however, the family model characteristic of the peasant-elite society of the Middle Ages persisted as the valued role relation between clergy and laity. This persistence generated problems of dependency and rebellion that characterize certain parish experiences today and give rise to pressures to redefine legitimate clergy-laity relations by the Church.[30]

Concern about Social Justice: An Immanent Emphasis

Certain questions present themselves: why were not more of the spiritual energies of Catholics spontaneously turned toward the conditions of the social order during the centuries of transcendent emphasis? What controlled these spiritual energies to the extent that they were riveted on final causes or expended in charitable efforts which, though tremendous in their scope, never effectively challenged the injustices built into the very structure of the social order, and, on the contrary, rather took the social order as a given?

William Ferree's analysis in *The Act of Social Justice* helps to answer the question of how it was that, despite the doctrine of love of neighbor and the early tradition of the Church acting to reform social systems, the principle of *laissez faire* and the exploitations of

[29] For an understanding of the process of structural differentiation see Neil Smelser, *Social Change in the Industrial Revolution* (Chicago: University of Chicago Press, 1959).

[30] Michonneau, *Revolution in a City Parish* and Gerken, *Toward a Theology of the Layman.*

colonialism, for example, were countenanced; and why, except for enormous charitable efforts to relieve the indigent, the injustices structured in the social system went relatively unchallenged by an ethical evaluation from the Church. Ferree in analyzing the encyclicals of Pope Pius XI demonstrates that they contain for the first time a clarification of the Christian obligation to bring the social order into line with the norms of morality. He clarifies the fact that vice can be as well organized as virtue and challenges the assumption that what is evil is therefore disorganized.[31] The burden of Ferree's thesis is this: The teachings of St. Thomas have guided the selection of content for books on ethics and moral theology in seminaries and Catholic universities for the past six centuries. St. Thomas, building on the ethics of Aristotle, stressed the primacy of obedience and especially obedience to law. Even though, unlike Aristotle, he recognized that the law of the polity was itself subservient to the common good, still he so idealized the Greek *polis* type government that he did not handle the question of what man should do if the social organizations in which he plays roles are structured in injustice.[32] Because he did not handle it, (and we can add because the vigilance of the Church over public order declined in this next era), in the next six centuries seminarians and Catholic university students trained in the Thomistic tradition received much clarification of their duties in individual justice and the perfecting of the right intention but little in how to handle the problem of structured evil.[33] By the twentieth century this had resulted in such extreme formalism in theological and philosophical training that Pope Pius XI had to make explicit that a good intention is not enough to fulfill a Christian obligation in justice. Rather, man must not only have the intention of doing good, but must also acquire the necessary information, training, and programming to effect the good end desired. This leads him to state that "A constant and serious preoccupation with social organization in all its forms and in all its

[31] Ferree, *The Act of Social Justice*, pp. 110-11, 186.

[32] *Ibid.*, pp. 25, 80-81, 111-12. On this point see also Jacques Leclercq, *Christians in the World*, trans. Kathleen Pond (New York: Sheed & Ward, 1958). Here Leclercq explores the source of the focus on individual and on social morality.

[33] Ferree, *The Act of Social Justice*, pp. 80, 111 and Congar, *Lay People in the Church*, p. 20.

levels is the duty according to his capacity of every man living in society."[34]

This emphasis of Pope Pius XI as described by Ferree not only involves responsibility for the social order but also requires new attitudes towards science and the intellectual life for the development of the necessary expertise. It implies a whole new orientation toward secular society measured strictly in terms of the common good.

FREEDOM AND JUSTICE—
FOCUS OF PRESSURES TO CHANGE

These two new developments in the Church, (1) a re-evaluation of role relations of the laity and clergy in the work of the Church and in the community, (2) the obligation of the Christian in justice to bring the social order into conformity with the common good—both of which stem so clearly from the Christian responsibility to love all men—would not be receiving these reconsiderations had not serious pressures from within and outside the Church urged these reforms. Any institutionalized set of norms will continue to be taught, and deviations from them will continue to be sanctioned, until there is clear evidence that they are questionable means for achieving the ultimate goals of the system. That currently institutionalized practices in some areas are no longer functional is clear from the European studies of declining Church attendance and from surveys of belief.[35] The condition of the Church as an institution in South America and in the colonial areas now in transition is further evidence. In America the problem is not so evident, but it exists. The alienation of the worker and the intellectual from the Church on the Continent is a dominant concern in France at the present time. The growing search for meaning in thought systems like existential phenomenology and logical positivism on the intellectual side, and systems of social reform like Communism and other forms of religiously alienated socialism on the social welfare side, currently challenges the adequacy of the

[34] Ferree, *The Act of Social Justice*, p. 110.
[35] Michonneau, *Revolution in a City Parish*. See also Iraneus Rosier, *I Looked for God's Absence*, trans. Ilona Ricardo (New York: Sheed & Ward, 1960).

Christian purpose of finding the ultimate meaning of all things in God and of seeking Him through service to others.[36]

THE EFFECT OF PROLONGED TRANSCENDENT
EMPHASIS—THE PROBLEM OF GOD

Secular humanists of the last century in the social sciences alone, from Hegel through Feuerbach, Marx, Nietzsche, to Freud, have questioned the institutionalized patterns of interpersonal relations within the Church in every one of the five areas examined here. They have traced the inadequacies to the inability of the Christian ethic to effect the making of a social order in which all men can be free to work out their potential and achieve happiness.[37] In each case they have found the institutionalized idea of God inhibiting human freedom and behavior stemming from the Christian commitment inadequate from the point of view of social justice. Yet it was not until the secular humanist challenged the very existence of God and the effectiveness of the Church's social programs and was listened to by the masses that the adaptation-oriented in the Church were heard by those committed to the currently institutionalized norms. The prophets in the Church discovered that frequently the idea of God being taught in the local Church is an inadequate explanation of the relationship between God and man in the light of what is now known from science and philosophy about reality. Yet it is this inadequate idea of God that is in many cases legitimating the institutionalized relations between the Church on earth and the rest of mankind.[38] Such a discovery has stimulated penetrating new philosophical and theological treatises which, in turn, provoke within the system search-

[36] See Albert Dondeyne, *Contemporary European Thought and Christian Faith*, trans. Ernan McMullin and John Burnheim (Pittsburgh, Pa.: Duquesne University, 1958), pp. 39-40 and Peter Riga, *Catholic Thought in Crisis* (Milwaukee, Wis.: Bruce Publishing Co., 1963).

[37] See, for example, Hegel, *The Philosophy of History*; Ludwig A. Feuerbach, *The Essence of Christianity*, trans. George Eliot (New York: Harper & Row, Publishers, 1957); Friedrich Wilhelm Nietzsche, *Beyond Good and Evil* (Chicago: Henry Regnery Co. for the Great Books Foundation, 1949); and Sigmund Freud, *The Future of an Illusion*, trans. W. D. Robson-Scott (New York: Anchor Books, Doubleday & Company, Inc., 1957).

[38] M. D. Chenu and Friedrich Heer, "Is the Modern World Atheist?" *Cross Currents*, XI, No. 1 (1961), 5-24.

ing examination of existing institutions at this very critical level.[39] Albert Dondeyne, professor of philosophy at Louvain University, observes at the conclusion of *Contemporary European Thought and Christian Faith:*

> It is by no means a simple task to reconcile belief in a Divine immutable revelation with a healthy and vigorous humanism that respects the historical character of human life. The bringing together of time and eternity and more important, the entry of the eternal into history (which is, after all, the essence of the Christian religion, centered as it is around the true mystery of the Incarnation of God) pose multiple problems both in theory and practice. Is historicity consistent with the existence of an Absolute outside history, an Absolute which is yet in constant relation with history?[40]

This statement by a leading contemporary philosopher in the Church indicates the extent to which the present pressures to change are rooted in the very conception of God on the one hand and the need for a transition in emphasis from transcendence to immanence on the other. All seem to agree with Cardinal Suhard that "the greatest fault of Christians in the 20th Century would be to leave the world to shape itself and bring itself to unity without them."[41]

A PARADIGM OF THE CULTURAL BASE OF
THE PRESSURES TO CHANGE

In order to clarify in sociological terms how these historical factors and the current pressures to change are related to the social structure of the Church, the following paradigm (Table 2.1) was constructed. It relates the pressures to change to basic Christian values grounded in the belief system (column 1) by specifying which institutionalized norms have been so emphasized in the past (column 2) that certain interpersonal relations reinforced by the norms (column 3) have in time become dysfunctional for achieving the goals of the system and are now criticized as strain areas, in view of current need for different behaviors more functionally related to

[39] See *Cross Currents*, XII, No. 2 (1962), entire issue.
[40] P. 140.
[41] Emmanuel Cardinal Suhard, quoted in *ibid.*, p. 189.

table 2.1
RELATION OF VALUES, NORMS, STRAINS, AND PRESSURES TO CHANGE CHARACTERISTIC OF THE SOCIAL STRUCTURE OF THE CHURCH AS INSTITUTIONALIZED IN THE LOCAL COMMUNITY

Valued doctrinal base	Institutionalized norm	Behavior for which change is recommended	Social-psychological norm for community effectiveness
1. God is the Father	Locus of authority is in God and His representatives on earth	Authoritarian submission and rebellion (O'Dea, Murray, Congar)[a]	Leader-follower resiliency (Nietzsche)
2. Man's ultimate goal is eternal salvation	The primary vocation for man involves withdrawal from the world	Lack of social responsibility in the work situation and in the local community (Ferree, Cogley, McEoin)	Social responsibility (Marx)
3. Conformity to the will of God is the ideal for all human behavior	Emphasis on obedience in child training	Overdependency in adult relations (O'Dea, Weigel)	Independence training in child rearing (Piaget)
4. Prayer is man's way of communicating with God	In all difficulties man should turn to God in prayer	Negative attitude toward the scientific method (McMullin, Tavard, Ellis)	Respect for the intellectual life (Weber)
5. Man is made in the image and likeness of God	Emphasis on the intellect and will; de-emphasis on the lower appetites in ethical training	Negative attitude toward the understanding of the unconscious (Hagmaier, Cogley, O'Dea)	Motivational awareness (Freud)

[a] The names refer to authors who have stressed this strain item or social-psychological norm.

modern exigencies (column 4). In the paradigm the many voices out-side the Church pressuring for change are identified by a prototype for each strain area: Nietzsche for the command-obedience issue; Marx for social responsibility; Piaget for independence training for children; Max Weber for respect for the intellectual life; and Freud for motivational awareness. The relationships expressed in this diagram are derived from the basic assumptions of Parsons' analysis of social systems, which explains that patterns of interaction in social behavior are controlled by norms selected in time from many possible norms because of their functional usefulness but grounded in values that constitute the belief system, and that this relationship of behaviors in roles to norms and values constitutes a cybernetic system.[42] It follows that although norms are originally selected for their functional effectiveness, it is the values grounded in ultimate meaning and belief systems which set the limits on the forms that norms can legitimately take. Behaviors in conformity with these norms are reinforced by the reward-punishment system and so become internalized through the socialization process, thus setting the characteristic style of behavior in a given sociocultural setting. When, in the course of time, institutionalized normative patterns become too narrow in emphasis to meet new functional exigencies, pressures to change create psychological strains around the behaviors conforming to these now dysfunctional normative controls. Although many other norms might be equally reflective of commitment to the same basic values, criticisms of normative patterns are interpreted by some as threats to the organizational structure of the system itself. If one perceives the system's meanings to be embodied in the norms, such criticism is a threat. But if the system's meaning is perceived as essentially in the values, there is no threat, since values can legitimate other norms besides those currently institutionalized. This diagram was prepared by working back from the strain areas to the values and norms that seem to be related to them. It links the historical groundings of the present strains with the transcendent emphasis in the historical analysis and helps explain the logic of current thinkers in the Church who are urging change in the five areas.

[42] Parsons *et al.*, *Theories of Society*, I (New York: Free Press of Glencoe, Inc., 1961), pp. 37-38.

SOURCES OF EVIDENCE

The five areas of pressures to change were selected after a three-year study of reputable Catholic scholar-writers who were intimating that currently institutionalized practices were not fulfilling the intended functions of the Catholic Church. These observations, made predominantly by priests trained especially in theology and philosophy, taken together with statements by a laity trained in the social sciences and in the humanities, fell into strikingly similar areas.[43] The five topics categorized as command-obedience relations,

---

[43] Many of the writers whose works will be referred to in this analysis are better known in Europe than in America: Yves Congar, O.P., a major Catholic spokesman on ecclesiology in France; Emmanuel Cardinal Suhard, Archbishop of Paris after World War II; Hans Küng, priest and professor of theology at the University of Tübingen; M. D. Chenu, O.P., historian of theology in France; Augustine Cardinal Bea, S.J., president of the Secretariat for promoting Christian Unity and for more than twenty-five years teacher at the Pontifical Biblical Institute in Rome; Maria Theresa Antonelli, professor of philosophy at the University of Genoa; Karl Rahner, S.J., theology teacher at the Jesuit seminary at Innsbruck; Marc Oraison, French priest and doctor of theology and medicine, and a psychiatrist; A. M. Dubarle, O.P., a Biblical specialist, professor of Scripture at Saulchoir; Pierre Teilhard de Chardin, S.J., a French anthropologist; Friedrich Heer, medieval historian in Belgium; Augustin-Pierre Léonard, O.P., professor at La Harte du Puy College in Belgium; Emmanuel Mounier, founder of the monthly review *Esprit* in France; Hans Urs von Balthasar, Swiss theologian and priest, author of studies on Barth, Origen, and Bernanos; Jean Daniélou, leader of Catholic biblical revival in France; Henri deLubac, S.J., professor of history of religions at Lyon-Fourviere in France; Jacques Maritain, the leading Neo-Thomist of today, and Albert Dondeyne, professor of philosophy at the University of Louvain.

Among the Americans are John Courtney Murray, S.J., theologian from the Jesuit seminary at Woodstock, Maryland; Monsignor John Tracy Ellis, professor of Church history at the Catholic University of America; the late Gustave Weigel, S.J., a leader in the ecumenical dialogue and theologian at Woodstock College; George Tavard, professor of theology at Mount Mercy College and leader of ecumenical thought in America; Gordon Zahn, sociologist from Loyola University, Chicago; Thomas O'Dea, sociologist from Fordham and the University of Utah; Thomas Merton, monk of the Cistercian Abbey at Gethsemane, Kentucky, and spiritual writer; H. A. Reinhold, priest and leader of the liturgical revival in America; Robert W. Gleason, S.J., chairman of the theology department of Fordham University; John Cogley, formerly editor of *Commonweal*, currently director of the Center for the Study of Democratic Institutions sponsored by the Fund for the Republic; and Daniel Callahan, associate editor of *Commonweal*.

social responsibility, independence training, respect for the intellectual life, and motivational awareness constantly repeated themselves.

An analysis of articles in *Cross Currents*[44] between Spring 1957 and Spring 1961 offered a check on completeness of coverage of problem areas that was even more systematic than the study of scholar-writers. Results verified that the five areas do, in fact, represent separate, repeated themes inclusive of most, if not all, of the value-based pressures-to-change patterns of interpersonal behavior reflected in the organizational structure in the Church at the present time.[45] No other major category was suggested for addition.

FIVE CATEGORIES OF PRESSURES TO CHANGE

Command-obedience Relations

There are those in the Church who feel that the Church currently faces serious problems of authority because of the persistence of certain traditional patterns of father-child relations. The problem expresses itself both in overconformity to and rebellion against authority. Gordon Zahn's *German Catholics and Hitler's Wars* is an example of the former and Rosier's *I Looked for God's Absence* of the latter. In a society in which the majority of people no longer live in small peasant communities, many established patterns of childlike obedience expectations no longer have the meaning they once had and no longer seem functional for carrying out the work of the Church. Today Church members live in constant interaction with others who do not share their commitments. They live in a society in which there has been and will continue to be a general upgrading of all classes of workers, in which universal education is becoming common and professional competence is increasing. Through mass communications the ordinary worker has contact with the major ideas of

[44] Published by Catholic laymen, and subtitled "a journal to study the impact of Christianity on our times," *Cross Currents* features translations, reprints, and original articles which critically and penetratingly re-examine what is currently institutionalized in the Church.

[45] "Value based" in distinction from "interest based." Here this refers to the fact that these criticisms stem from concern for the principles of Christianity rather than from protection of the special interests of the Church as institutionalized. Chapter Five will explain the choice of pressures to change from one rather than from both positions.

the times. He is expected to participate responsibly in the management of his business, his community, his local and national government. He can, if he wishes, participate in cultural and social activities that develop his abilities and expand his horizons. Simultaneously, the diffuse role characteristic of the priest in the peasant community has been delimited to priestly services: the Mass, the sacraments, public prayer, and preaching. Because of the secularization of the modern world and its upgrading, the gospel command "to teach all nations" is becoming more fully defined as an activity expected jointly of the laity, the rank-and-file priest, and the hierarchy. As a result, even in the work of the Church, the priest, though pastor of souls, is often fellow worker as well as father. Paternalism toward the citizen in the polity and toward the worker in industry had to be relinquished because of democratization and professionalization, so likewise it is being challenged in the clergy as they work for the salvation of the world.[46] The extensive literature on obedience in the Church suggests that within the Church the problem of obedience, as presented in such studies as the *Authoritarian Personality*,[47] is sufficiently pertinent to warrant warnings and urging to change.[48]

Behind this problem is the deeper issue of the proper relationship

[46] See Seymour M. Lipset, "Democracy and Working Class Authoritarianism," *American Sociological Review*, XXIV, No. 4 (1959), 482-501.

[47] See T. W. Adorno *et al.*, *The Authoritarian Personality* (New York: Harper & Row, Publishers, 1950). This study, springing from a desire to understand the anti-Semitism that permitted the genocide of Hitler's regime, describes a personality syndrome that is prone to submit unquestioningly to any demands of an established authority. The study is particularly concerned with the successful establishment of a fascist regime.

[48] Gordon Zahn, *German Catholics and Hitler's Wars* (New York: Sheed & Ward, 1962); Mother Mary Gallins, *The German Resistance to Hitler, Ethical and Religious Factors* (Washington, D.C.: Catholic University Press, 1961); Yves Congar, study of *Lay People in the Church*; Maria Antonelli, "The Cloister and the City: the Meaning of Obedience Today," *Cross Currents*, VIII, No. 2 (1958), 144-52; Daniel Callahan, "The Council and the Catholic," *Cross Currents*, VI, No. 2 (1962), 183-93; Daniel Callahan, *The Mind of the Catholic Layman* (New York: Charles Scribner's Sons, 1963); Hans Küng, *The Council, Reform, and Reunion*; Augustin-Pierre Léonard, O.P., "Freedom of the Laity," *Catholic Action Reprints* (Dayton, O.: University of Dayton, Reprint No. 178); Michael Novak, "The Priest in the Modern World," *Review for Religious*, XX (July, 1961), 265-71; Charles Taylor, "Clericalism," *Cross Currents*, X, No. 4 (1960), 327-36.

between God and man and the traditional perception of a kinship model of father and children roles. Psychological studies of man's tendencies, when anxious and afraid, to revert to childhood behavior (treating the other as the child does his parents) add further significance and demonstrate the need of a deeper understanding of the meaning of expected role relations in the Church. Thus the persistent problem of command-obedience relations also touches the area of motivational awareness.[49]

Social Responsibility

Social responsibility today is commonly considered as a problem of social justice. The question is whether or not Catholics are assuming their share of responsibility for making their communities reflect the principles of Christian ethics. In a basic sense this is the major issue in the whole pressure for change in the role of the Church facing the secular community. It is the evidence of the ineffectiveness of the gospel message in public life that urges change. The criticism implies that nothing specifically Christian distinguishes the behavior of Catholics from that of others of his social class who do not share his religiously grounded obligation to serve his neighbor as he would serve Christ.[50] The critics do not question the extraordinary services of some Christians. They are asserting that for living Christianity in Christ's way, what is being done today is not sufficient. They point out that the world is not being influenced by the social justice practiced by Catholics to as great an extent as it is influenced by the scandalous behavior of some Catholics in public office and private business and by the general social indifference of Christians to problems of integration, service to underdeveloped nations, and other forms of human service that the gospel expects of the Christian. In general, this second pressure for change, that of social responsibility, asks for more active

[49] See Eric Fromm, *Escape from Freedom* (New York: Farrar, Straus & Company, 1941) and Eric H. Erickson, *Childhood and Society* (New York: W. W. Norton & Company, Inc., 1950).

[50] W. W. Grossouw, *Spirituality of the New Testament*, pp. 151-52. Jacques Maritain, as early as 1938, stated that Communism is turned against belief because "it originates, chiefly through the fault of a Christian world unfaithful to its own principles." Jacques Maritain, *True Humanism* (London: Geoffrey Bles: The Century Press, 1938), p. 33.

participation in the making of a better world according to the Christian ideal of service to all mankind. It is a reprimand, too, of that Catholicism represented by a ghetto mentality or a complacent middle-class closed community, insensitive to the pressing needs of the deprived, the underprivileged, and the rejected. This reprimand exposes not so much a lack of charity as a neglect of basic social justice evidenced by toleration of social conditions, institutionalized, but evil.

Independence Training

Independence training focuses on developing the capacity of children to take responsibility so that later as adults they can participate responsibly in the community of business and in social life. Those pressing for change stress the need for training in initiative. They also hold that the capacity to accept criticism for one's failures and to respond with more creative effort is crucial for functioning in the interdependence of modern society. The problem in child training arises from a traditional emphasis on the fourth commandment— "Honor thy father and thy mother"—to the relative neglect of those other commandments that refer to a mature community life, the seventh—"thou shalt not steal," and the eighth—"thou shalt not bear false witness against thy neighbor." These latter, dealing with honesty and truthfulness, are basic to the structure of trust necessary for effective social organization. The criticism is not that these commandments have not been taught, but that in the overemphasis on obedience they were not absorbed in proper balance and hence are not reflected in adult behavior in public life and in business.

Closely associated with this problem is the type of discipline used in the home and in parochial schools, especially as it shapes attitudes towards work. This criticism observes that devotion to work as a "calling" which Max Weber describes in *The Protestant Ethic and the Spirit of Capitalism* would surprise many Catholics.[51] Congar has

[51] See Gerhard Lenski, *The Religious Factor, A Sociological Study of Religion's Impact on Politics, Economics and Family Life* (Garden City, N.Y.: Doubleday & Company, Inc., 1961), p. 83. See also M. D. Chenu, O.P., "Toward a Theology of Work," *Cross Currents*, VII, No. 2 (1957), 175-83. Richard Cardinal Cushing, in his Pastoral Letter for Lent 1962, entitled *The Call of the*

pointed out in his *Lay People in the Church* that the consideration of work as punishment for sin rather than as means to conquer the universe stems from an exclusive emphasis on the life hereafter, which, for many years, made preparation for life in this world only a minor concern of Church discipline. This attitude became so dominant that the whole field of work came to be perceived as secular and outside the discipline of Christian ethics.[52]

Respect for the Intellectual Life

Catholic attitudes toward the intellectual life generated the most dynamic of all the pressures to change. In 1955 Monsignor John Tracy Ellis started a flood of self-analysis among Catholics by issuing at the American Catholic Educational Association's national convention his criticism of the inadequacy of Catholic scholarship in the scientific, technological, and general intellectual fields.[53]

The amount of literature on the Catholic and the intellectual life has become so extensive in the past seven years that someone has called it "an orgy of self criticism."[54] Whole bibliographies on this topic are readily available. Already the criticism has stimulated indignant reactions from those Catholic centers of learning with a long tradition of excellence.[55] It has also initiated much serious education survey and upgrading.

Motivational Awareness

A pressure towards greater motivational awareness projects criticism against a tendency to minimize the role of unconscious motivation in human behavior. The writings of Freud, the work of

---

Council (Boston: Daughters of St. Paul, 1962), p. 32, urges a new approach to work as part of the Catholic apostolate in the community.

[52] Congar, *Lay People in the Church*, pp. 370, 413.

[53] John Tracy Ellis, "American Catholics and the Intellectual Life," *Thought*, XXX, No. 3 (1955), 351-88.

[54] Sister Joan Bland, S.N.D., *New Republic*, October 10, 1960, p. 28 (letter to the editor).

[55] Andrew M. Greeley has brought this list up to date to 1961 in his *Religion and Career: A Survey of College Graduates* (New York: Sheed & Ward, 1963). Father Greeley attempts to demonstrate that sociocultural factors rather than creed, code, and cult explain differences in performance between religious groups with different belief systems.

psychoanalytic therapists, and the subsequent failure of Church leaders to accept and use psychological findings have stimulated this criticism.[56] The most logical target of critics is rational psychology, a branch of Thomistic philosophy which emphasizes the intellect and will to the relative neglect of the functions of the emotions. Although emotions are analyzed in scholastic psychology, the stress is on man's capacity to control them by intellect and will, and the frequency with which the order of control is reversed tends to be ignored or at least not treated as common.[57]

The criticism shows that this traditional emphasis on man's rational capability, so common to Western education since the age of the enlightenment, has fostered some institutionalized practices that must be re-evaluated in the light of the findings of modern psychology. There is, for example, the tendency to talk about what ought to be so (because of the teaching of the Church) as if it were so in most cases. There is also the tendency to discount the high level of irrationality in human behavior; it is not seen as a problem needing serious consideration.

Studies of prejudice, however, underline the seriousness of this neglect of the irrational. They have revealed a high correlation between the rejection of minority groups and the highly conventional practice of religion with its naïve explanations of behavior.[58] Examination of several pieces of "hate" literature raises questions as to why the same themes are constantly associated: extreme patriotism, strong

[56] Catholic critics of the lack of motivational awareness include O'Dea in *The American Catholic Dilemma*, pp. 151-67; George Hagmaier and Robert Gleason, *Counseling the Catholic* (New York: Sheed & Ward, 1959); M. D. Chenu and Friedrich Heer, "Is the Modern World Atheist?" *Cross Currents*, XI, No. 1 (1961), 5-24; Marc Oraison, "The Psychoanalyst and the Confessor," *Cross Currents*, VIII, No. 4 (1958), 363-76; Gregory Zilboorg, *Psychoanalysis and Religion* (New York: Farrar, Straus & Company, Inc., 1962).

[57] Examine, for example, the following textbooks long used in rational psychology: Robert E. Brennan, *Thomistic Psychology* (New York: The Macmillan Company, 1941); Timothy J. Gannon, *Psychology, the Unity of Human Behavior* (Boston: Ginn & Company, 1954); Paul J. Glenn, *Psychology* (St. Louis, Mo.: B. Herder Book Company, 1936).

[58] See, for example, Gordon W. Allport, *The Nature of Prejudice* (New York: Doubleday & Company, Inc., 1958), pp. 418-25; Adorno *et al., The Authoritarian Personality*, pp. 733-43; and Milton Rokeach, *The Open and Closed Mind* (New York: Basic Books, 1960).

emphasis on Christianity, anti-Semitism, anti-integration, anti-aid to underdeveloped nations, and an anti-communism which constantly urges violent forms of destruction to annihilate the enemy. The 1962 phenomenon of large numbers of religiously committed middle-class people joining extremely conservative groups bent on punitive response to outgroups indicates how effectively religion can be used by those who are anxious—how it can be used as a way to preserve for themselves an island-of-safety by rejecting the stranger and by destroying the enemy,[59] a striking example of lack of motivational awareness.

HYPOTHESES FOR THE CURRENT SITUATION

After all these considerations of the historical groundings and the current pressures to change in the Church, the question still remains: how much change will these pressures effect in the local communities to which they are fundamentally addressed? The hypothesis of this research is that they will not even be heard where the definition of the situation expressed in the commitment to the transcendent still has primacy and has not been broken through by any functional exigency which is felt in the local parish. Where there is cause for concern and dissatisfaction with the *status quo*, openness to change will be limited to the degree to which this new understanding of the place of immanence in the belief system of the Church is heard and understood. Where it has not been heard or discovered by probing analysis, and where there is still complacency with what is institutionalized, mechanisms of defense, styles of response, and the old definitions themselves will be used in recognizable ways to resist any inroads from new programs or any suggestions for change. These "recognizable ways" function in themselves to resist change.

For the purpose of investigation, it will be assumed here that the five strain areas exist within the Catholic community and (1) are dysfunctional, (2) are permitted in some areas to thrive because of existing norms within the Church, and (3) would be a matter of concern for treatment and reform if they could be perceived objectively as emergents from currently institutionalized norms without threat to the basic structure of belief.

[59] See, for example, Robert A. Graham, "The John Birch Society," *America*, December 2, 1961, pp. 324-29.

Those who want the existing norms to change and who cannot differentiate between them and the basic beliefs, instead of resorting to mechanisms and other forms of adjustment, can, in a straightforward or indirect way, simply leave the Church. These people will not effect change in the system but will join other social systems or start new sects or simply become alienated. This group is not examined in this study. They require a separate treatment.

THE SAMPLE AND EXTRAPOLATION

The sample to be examined in this study consists of priests of the Boston archdiocese active in the parish and in diocesan administrative work. Why and how they were chosen will be discussed in Chapter Four. Two major problems, however, present themselves immediately: (1) A priest in his role in the local community faces stimuli to change. Is his stance of sufficient magnitude in the historical process so that from a study of it we may move to generalizations about the course of history? (2) Is the change process that occurs in religious organizations relevant to change in other social systems where relations between values and social structure is much less explicit, if it is present at all?

It is important to raise these questions at this time in order to keep the theoretical problem in focus. Concerning the second question it can be said that at present there seem to be no comparable studies aimed at determining how orientation to values, interests, and change manifested at one time affects response to stimuli to change presented at a later date. If the findings of this study can be shown to have relevance to other historically grounded situations now facing stimuli to change, then this study can easily be replicated in other areas with parallel research instruments. With reference to the first question this chapter has attempted to demonstrate that these stimuli are historically grounded. The use of stimuli not artificially created, but actually selected from the on-going historical process, more realistically grounded than laboratory data and less impersonal than the survey, is itself justification of the object of analysis.

3

measuring orientations to values, interests, and change
The problem proposed in this research on the function of values and interests in the process of social change is an attempt to account for discrepancies between Marxian and Parsonian explanations of social change. The Church in the local community is taken as the object of analysis because it is presently facing pressures to change that have roots in history. This fulfills the necessary condition for the theoretical issue, namely, that the experimental situation be itself a part of the historical process. This chapter briefly describes the instrument by which significant role players were selected for participation in the study.[1]

THE MEASURING PROBLEM

Because no standard method exists for measuring orientations to values, interests, and change, development of such a measuring instrument was imperative. The two basic propositions to describe people in social roles facing stimuli to change have already been established in Chapter One. The first indicated the two general orientations to making choice, one called a value orientation: a tendency to

[1] The method is assumed to be one way of operationalizing the propositions about the role of values in structure and in change in social systems, as found in Marx's and Parsons' sociology.

be guided by principles more general than the given situation; the other an interest orientation: a tendency to making a choice in terms of one's own ties with the people in the situation. The second proposition dealt with the tendency to resist or to be open to change. Preparatory considerations suggested that responses to stimuli to change would be conditioned by these orientations and that the responses as well as the stimuli themselves were important determinants of the direction of the historical process.

Now it becomes necessary to classify the respondents in terms of their degree of openness to change and their tendency to use values or interests as the criterion of choice in situations involving the larger community. Even the assumption that such a classification is reflective of the real world was itself problematic and part of the problem under consideration. Much experimentation preceded the formulation of the final draft of the instrument which, in its present form, though still not completely satisfying, gives striking evidence of measuring something that explains differences in styles of response to change-oriented stimuli. In order to understand its purpose, it will be necessary to examine the theoretical base from which it was developed.

From what has been said in Chapter One it would seem that everyone has values, standards of excellence, in terms of which certain objectives remain primary while others are less important. Everyone, too, has interests, inner urges to move toward some end as it promises satisfaction for the self or for one's group. To what degree these standards of excellence and inner urges make differences in social structure is very difficult to determine. Two questions are pertinent: (1) Are values regularly subjected to distortion, manipulation, reinterpretation to fit more dynamic unconscious or conscious pressures for action such as needs, desires, or functional exigency? (2) Or are values relatively stable elements that function to set limits to the variations of choice permitted an individual as he functions in his social roles?[2] Of all the possible aspects of the value-interest-change problem that could be explored, the one that stimulated this study is the examination of the relationship between these two questions on the one hand and orientation to change on the other. The study assumes that both values and interests operate in every case but that

[2] This is a reformulation of the Marx-Parsons difference in explaining the essential role of values in social systems discussed in Chapter One, pp. 3-7.

individuals differ in the extent of their response to the guiding function of the one and the driving force of the other. The task, then, in
devising a measuring instrument was to capture these orientations to
values, interest, change, and nonchange. But how can one get spontaneous definitions of situations in areas of change, nonchange, values,
and interests? Can this be done in a way consistent enough to warrant
calling the findings stable characteristics grounded either in personality, or in social system factors, or in some complex combination
of these imbedded in specific situations?

A few years ago in their study of the soviet system, Kluckhohn,
Inkeles, and Bauer touched a relevant point:

> It is a commonplace of psychology that the outlook of any group
> upon the world and experiences is determined and reflected to an impor-
> tant extent by the clichés they continually use, by the habitual premises
> which they accept.[3]

This constitutes an enriched form of Thomas' definition of the situation statement that "If men define a situation as real it is real in its
consequence," and gives a clear suggestion of the kind of item one
might develop for measuring different orientations to change, values,
and interests—the cliché. Clichés are frequently heard and can easily
be collected. By writing cliché-type items and asking subjects if they
accept or reject them, one can get measures of orientation to the
content.

Several studies to date have developed effective measuring instruments that seem to get at underlying attitudes and feeling tone and to
reach a rather clear definition of the way things are perceived. The
best known of these include the F test in *The Authoritarian Personality* study,[4] the instrument Rokeach uses in *The Open and Closed
Mind*,[5] and, more particularly, the Value Profile developed by Bales
and Couch.[6] Already there is substantial evidence that these instruments distinguish among people who perceive the world differently in
certain areas and respond accordingly. Since the first instrument

[3] Raymond Bauer, Alex Inkeles, and Clyde Kluckhohn, *How the Soviet
System Works* (Cambridge, Mass.: Harvard University Press, 1959), p. 166.

[4] Adorno *et al.*, *The Authoritarian Personality*, pp. 77-83.

[5] Rokeach, *The Open and Closed Mind*, pp. 71-97.

[6] Robert F. Bales and Arthur S. Couch. Copies of this instrument are
available from the Laboratory of Social Relations, Social Relations Department,
Harvard University.

needed in this study performs a similar function of differentiating people according to their orientations toward certain variables, the style of item used here and the method for selecting the items were modeled on these earlier instruments. They all use cliché-type items.

THE CONTENT OF THE INITIAL MEASURING INSTRUMENT

One hundred and twenty cliché-like statements expressing attitudes toward change, values, and interests were formulated from suggestions culled from spontaneous remarks, current periodicals, other attitude scales, and more formal literary sources. These were administered to several pretest samples for which the subjects were chosen because of their conservative or liberal orientations (as judged by their peers). Sixty items were selected, fifteen for each of the four orientations—change, nonchange, values, and interests. The selection was made in favor of those items that best discriminated between known conservative and liberal subjects.[7] The final form of the questionnaire was then administered to a random sample of priests of the diocese of Boston. Two hundred and fifty-nine priests or 70 per cent of the number sampled returned completed forms. While this chapter is devoted to the analysis of the content of the orientation measure in an effort to describe the meaning of what was measured, whenever tables are introduced, the figures refer to the responses of this group, or, where specified, to the pretest group. Table 3.1 is presented to give a brief picture of the types of items used and the differences in discriminatory powers of the various items.[8]

[7] Subjects for the pretest were selected priests from different religious orders including Jesuits, Dominicans, and Paulists. Other samples included college students, parish groups, and women religious. In each case, the orientation to change was known before the subject was chosen.

[8] In Table 3.1, "DP Pretest" refers to the discriminatory power of the items when given to a pretest sample of 50 priests, lay people, and women religious. The "Sample" refers to the 259 priests of the diocese who answered the questionnaire. The discriminatory power (DP) is a measure to determine whether or not the item distinguished between high and low scorers on the variable being measured. For a description of how it was used here, see Adorno *et al.*, *The Authoritarian Personality*, pp. 80-83. According to this source a DP of approximately 2 indicates that the item was chosen more by high scorers than by low scorers in the general area being measured, that is, change, nonchange, values, or interests. A full copy of the instrument will be found in the Appendix.

table 3.1

EXAMPLES OF ITEMS USED TO DETERMINE ORIENTATIONS TO VALUE, INTEREST, CHANGE, AND NONCHANGE

Number of Item	DP Sample[a]	DP Pretest
Interest Items		
1. The best way to improve world conditions is for each man to take care of his own corner of the vineyard.	2.34	3.13
2. In times of crisis, it is only natural for men to think of themselves first even though they may be ashamed of it afterwards.	2.24	2.12
3. Man is not an idealist by nature. It is hard for him not to be motivated primarily by self-interest.	2.14	2.66
Value Items		
4. Concerns about caution have little place when the issue is one of social justice.	2.14	3.20
5. When I hear of people who are deprived of freedom and of just treatment, I really get involved; I find myself planning how I can help them.	2.47	3.50
6. When I am dealing with the problems of my own job, I find myself constantly trying to make decisions that will help to solve the bigger issues of justice, etc., for all mankind. The world's problems are very much my problems.	2.73	2.89
Change Items		
7. The current situation in the Church calls for change. We must respond at once.	2.78	2.41
8. There is really something refreshing about enthusiasm for change.	2.02	—
9. The Church in her teaching must adapt to the findings of science and modern exigencies.	2.02	2.95
Nonchange Items		
10. The future is in God's hands. I will await what He sends and accept what He sends as His will for me.	3.01	2.31

table 3.1 *continued*

11. In the final analysis the strongest basis for planning the future is to trust to the experience of the past and base the decision making on the facts, the historical facts.	2.65	2.02
12. Not change, but permanency and stability are what we are aiming for in the work of the Church.	2.37	2.34

ᵃ *"DP" refers to the "discriminatory power" of the item. See footnote 8.*

Within each of the four sets of items there are several different but related themes. Each item picked up some aspect of these themes which altogether define what is here called an interest, or value, or change, or nonchange orientation. The following outline records these themes.

The interest set
    a. Self-interest is natural.
    b. Action should be accompanied by caution.
    c. Individual action is better than social action.
    d. Action that ignores the power elite is futile.

The value set
    a. Social values prompt action.
    b. Values shape society.
    c. The subject is conscious of the values he holds.

The change set
    a. There is need for change right now.
    b. There is perennial need for change.
    c. The subject appreciates change.
    d. The subject is aware that man himself initiates change.

The nonchange set
    a. The past is good.
    b. Man should not initiate change.
    c. Change is dangerous.
    d. The eternal is now.

SPECIFICATION FOR ITEMS

The items were deliberately designed to avoid specificity with reference to particularly valued areas.[9] This specificity will be provided by the value-oriented stimuli to change included in the interview schedule which comprises the second part of this study.[10] Because value statements sound so "right" that it is easy to agree with them, these items were the most difficult to formulate in ways that would actually discriminate between value- and interest-oriented people. Many of the original set of value items had to be rejected because, despite good meaning content, they failed to discriminate between "highs" and "lows." The following item illustrates this point.

For creating a better world wherein justice, peace, freedom, responsibility, and charity would have real meaning far beyond anything we now imagine, I think man could do so much more than he is now doing.

Everybody could accept this item. Perhaps this is so because it asks or expects no personal commitment to action on the part of the respondent. Items like the following two, that demand action from the one who agrees with them, were more discriminating:

When I hear of people who are deprived of freedom and of just treatment, I really get involved; I find myself planning how I can help them. (DP 2.47)

and

When I am dealing with the problems of my own job, I find myself constantly trying to make decisions that will help solve the bigger issues of justice, etc., for all mankind. The world's problems are very much my problems. (DP 2.73)

The reason these two items are more discriminating seems to be that they require the individual to go beyond the statement of the plati-

[9] Justice and freedom are the only values specifically mentioned in the orientation instrument. These two are used widely in a Christian context as in the Ten Commandments and in *Pacem in Terris* (Glen Rock, N.J.: Paulist Press, 1963), Paragraph 149, Part V.
[10] See Chapter Five.

tude, and man finds it hard to accept them if he is doing nothing about the situation.

TABULATION

Scores were determined by rating each response from −3 to +3 depending on whether the subject strongly disagreed, disagreed, slightly disagreed, did not answer (zero score), agreed slightly, agreed, or agreed strongly. These scores were summed for each of the four variables, values, interest, change, and nonchange. Then the absolute distance between the change and nonchange scores and the value and interest scores was determined. These two numbers became the subject's final score, each marked according to which of the two variables concerned was more positive.

An example will best explain how this tabulation was done. One priest consistently agreed strongly with almost every value item while disagreeing with almost every interest item. Since there were 15 value items, the highest score he could possibly get on value would be 3 times 15, and the highest rejecting score he could give interest was 3 times 15. Had he cleared a perfect score, he would have had a +45 on value and a −45 on interest, totaling 90 for his final score, which would be labeled a value score, since value was the positive score. His actual score was 85 for value and 84 for change, since he also responded with a +3 on almost every change item and a −3 on every nonchange item. This was an unusually high score both for its size and its consistency. If a man had a +5 for value and a +15 for interest, his score would be assigned as 10 for interest, because the distance between 5 and 15 is 10, and interest is the more positive score. So also if he had a −8 for change and a −10 for nonchange, he would receive a score of 2 for change, since this is the more positive score.

Table 3.2 shows the total number of respondents in each category. Here it can be seen that only 12 subjects could not be classified into one of the four categories of VC, IC, VNC, and INC, because they had a zero score on one factor, having chosen equally in both directions. Some other scores were also quite low. (Appendix 1, page 165 lists the actual scores of the high- and low-ranking respondents in

table 3-2

DISTRIBUTION OF SCORES ON THE ORIENTATION TO VALUE-CHANGE, INTEREST-CHANGE, VALUE-NONCHANGE, AND INTEREST-NONCHANGE, FOR THE SAMPLE OF PRIESTS FROM THE ARCHDIOCESE OF BOSTON

Orientation Score	Number of Respondents	Per Cent
VC	91	35
IC	28	11
VNC	55	21
INC	73	28
0 scores	12[a]	5
Total	259	100

[a] *These 12 scores do not fit into any of the four categories. In each case the scores on value and interest or on change and nonchange were exactly alike so that together they equaled 0. Combined, they constitute a residual category.*

each category. This gives some idea of the actual range of scores.)[11] It remains to be seen from the analysis of the census data (Chapter Four) and from the actual experiment with pressures to change (Chapters Five to Nine) whether these scores have any meaning when subjects are classified this way at one point in time and some months later are presented with stimuli to change.[12]

[11] With the output from a 7090 IBM program, which yielded correlations of each item with every other item plus means and standard deviations, it was possible to analyze in detail the patterns of response. Some of the results of this analysis can be found on Appendix Table 2, page 166. The program was written with the assistance of Will Sepetowski and Father Paul Facey, S.J. Further analysis of the patterns of "Yea" saying and "Nay" saying will be analyzed in a later article. They yield a special kind of pattern independent of this study.

[12] The effort to measure attitudes and to consider the meaning of intervals between responses has a long history. The most complete analysis of all aspects of this issue can still be found in Burt Green's "Attitude Measurement," *Handbook of Social Psychology*, ed. Gardiner Lindzey (Cambridge, Mass.: Addison-Wesley Publishing Co., Inc., 1954), I, 335-69.

4

the diocesan clergy: sample and target population

In the spring of 1961 the questionnaire measuring orientations to values, interests, and change was mailed to a random stratified sample of one-fourth (367) the clergy of the Archdiocese of Boston. The priests whose orientations are the research concern of this study belong to an archdiocese whose unique history and setting constitute a critical part of the development of the Catholic Church in America. A brief historical sketch of the Archdiocese of Boston will clarify how the broad pressures to change already described are related to the particular history of the Church in this section of New England. It will also facilitate understanding the interview content to be presented in Chapters Five through Nine.

HIGHLIGHTS OF DIOCESAN HISTORY

The Archdiocese of Boston is one of the oldest dioceses in the United States. It was founded in 1808 just nineteen years after the establishment of the first diocese of Baltimore, of which it was originally a part. Through the nineteenth century it received contingents of all those immigrant groups that have not only created the style of Catholicism in America, but have also been perceived as problems by the original predominantly Protestant Anglo-Saxon population. The Irish, German, Italian, Polish, and French-Canadians, all of whom are represented in the diocese, are among the largest groups of immigrants with a Catholic cultural heritage. In the early days, a predominantly Irish immigration to the Boston diocese generated the local non-Catholic custom of using the words Irish and Catholic interchangeably when discussing the Catholic Church in America.[1] Immigration since the turn of the century, however, has brought Catholics from southern and, more recently, from eastern Europe, while the past decade shows an increase in Spanish-speaking immigrants of Catholic background. In the course of time, segments of these nationalities and others have come to the Boston area making the problem of the Church in New England a problem of cultural assimilation not only between the Church and the once predominantly Protestant local community, but among the various national groups within the Church. Even today the custom of establishing churches by language groups persists, though to a diminishing extent. Although assimilation proceeds quite rapidly, some local parishes, once predominantly Irish or Italian or French in population, even now perceive the infiltration of other groups as a violation of an integration they cherished as their own.

Despite varied nationality types, the predominance of Irish among the higher clergy, a historical characteristic of the Church in America,[2] is particularly evident in the Boston diocese. This factor reinforces the specter of "Irish Catholic power" so vividly painted by Paul Blanshard.[3] Distaste for Irish power was a dominant reason for the tendency of the old American stock to interpret increase in Catholic immigration as a threat to the American way of life. The activity of some Protestants in the Ku Klux Klan, the Know-Nothing Party, and

---

[1] For (1) sympathetic, (2) neutral, and (3) negative analyses of this situation see (1) John Tracy Ellis, *American Catholicism* (Chicago: University of Chicago Press, 1956); (2) Robert D. Cross, *The Emergence of Liberal Catholicism in America* (Cambridge, Mass.: Harvard University Press, 1958); (3) Paul Blanshard, *The Irish and Catholic Power* (Boston: The Beacon Press, 1953), respectively. For an excellent discussion of the early immigration to Boston see Oscar Handlin's *Boston's Immigrants*, 2nd ed. rev. (Cambridge, Mass.: Harvard University Press, 1959).

[2] See John Donovan, "The American Catholic Hierarchy: A Social Profile," *American Catholic Sociological Review*, XIX, No. 2 (1958), 98-112.

[3] *The Irish and Catholic Power.*

the American Protective Association generated hostilities that still function in the background of relations between the Churches in the New England area, even though they constitute but a dim memory for many non-natives. The negative image of the Catholic Church, where it persists, is a perception of Catholics as civically unconcerned, politically exploitative, negatively oriented toward work, permissive to impulse release in drinking, gambling, and aggression.[4] The changing Catholic population has reacted variously to this persisting image which still captures real aspects of an immigrant community described in Edwin O'Connor's *The Last Hurrah* and Thomas O'Dea's *American Catholic Dilemma*. These three sociological factors: (1) extensive and eclectic Catholic immigration from Europe, (2) predominance of Irish backgrounds among the higher clergy, (3) organization of hostile groups to oppose Catholic infiltration, are frequently cited in the interviews as part of the explanation of the current relationship between Catholics and others in the local community.

In 1789 what is now the Archdiocese of Boston was part of Bishop Carroll's see, which extended from Maine to the Gulf of Mexico and west to the Mississippi. Father Thayer, a native of the city, was the pastor of the first Catholic Church opened in Boston in 1790. The population was then 18,030 and the Catholics numbered 100. In 1800 there were only 1,200 Catholics in and around Boston, yet in 1808 it was made an episcopal see with Cheverus as the first Bishop. He was one of the priests forced to leave France because of the revolution. The first priest ordained in Boston, in 1817, was an Irishman, Father Dennis Ryan. The diocesan seminary opened in 1831, when there were eight priests and sixteen churches. The diocesan newspaper, *The Pilot*, began publication in 1829 under the title, *The Jesuit*. The outbreaks of hostility against Catholics began in 1829 and climaxed in the burning of the Ursuline convent in Charlestown in 1834. Irish Catholics were the dominant target, and dictatorship from Rome was the great fear. By 1835, shortly before the major immigrations began, there were 40,182 Catholics, 27 priests, and 22 churches in the diocese.

---

[4] For these negative descriptions see: Paul Blanshard, *American Freedom and Catholic Power* (Boston: The Beacon Press, 1949) and Edwin O'Connor's *The Last Hurrah* (Boston: Little, Brown & Co., 1956), which captures for posterity the local stereotype of the Irish politician in positive and negative tones.

By 1845, the Catholic population had increased to 53,000. In 1908, the centenary year, there were 800,000 Catholics, 45 per cent of the population of the Boston area.[5]

In 1963 the diocese of Boston, 2,465 square miles, extended through Essex, Norfolk, Middlesex, Suffolk, and Plymouth counties in the state of Massachusetts. The priests numbered 2,461 of whom 1,335 were diocesan clergy and 1,126 members of religious orders. A total of 5,968 sisters were teaching, doing social work, or living in contemplative retreat houses. There were in the diocese 408 parishes and 22 missions, 127 different orders of priests, brothers, and sisters, and 6 colleges, 243 elementary schools, and 99 high schools altogether serving 166,288 students. Other social services included 33 social, health, and community services besides 12 hospitals and 19 homes for the aged, children, and the convalescent. A diocesan major and minor seminary and 8 religious order houses granted degrees. The Catholic population at 1,733,620 was, in 1963, 50 per cent of the total population.[6] Clustered in the central city for some years, Catholics were now moving out to the suburbs in large numbers. Many towns on the South and North shores, once predominantly Protestant, had become predominantly Catholic in the previous ten years.

DRAWING AND REACHING THE SAMPLE

The research universe of these diocesan priests (excluding those who were teachers, Eastern rite clerics, and members of religious orders) numbered 1,228.[7] A sample of 367, more than one-fourth of

[5] The statistics for this section are taken from Michael J. Scanlan, *A Brief History of the Archdiocese of Boston* (Boston: Nicholas M. Williams Co., 1908). For a complete and richly documented history of the archdiocese of Boston see Robert H. Lord, John E. Sexton, and Edward T. Harrington, *History of the Archdiocese of Boston in the Various Stages of Its Development 1604-1943* (New York: Sheed & Ward, 1944).

[6] The percentage estimate here is determined from the census report for Essex, Norfolk, Middlesex, Suffolk, and Plymouth counties over the estimated Catholic population for the diocese.

[7] The question of whom to include generated several problems. (1) There were in 1960 in the diocese 2,212 priests, 1,228 of whom were diocesan, and 984 members of religious orders. Priests of religious orders were eliminated because their rule of life, vows, and training add uncontrolled variables. (2) The Eastern rite churches, retaining the Byzantine ritual and foreign languages, were also eliminated because the interpersonal relations and community contacts of

the universe, was selected by random-sampling procedures after stratification by age and type of parish.[8] The randomness was necessary to assure that the results (*a*) would be reflective of the total diocese and (*b*) could be related by statistical measure to the orientation scores.

Contacting the sample posed a problem because, containing both the orientation scale and several pages of questions on background data, the questionnaire was quite long. Mailing meant running the well-known risk of poor returns and incomplete responses.[9] These

---

these church members present a singular picture diverging markedly from the general diocesan pattern and requiring special study at the present time.

[8] The median age for the diocese was computed from the *Boston Catholic Directory*, which lists the year of ordination. Assuming that most priests are ordained about age twenty-six, we determined the actual age. (All the statistical computation was done with the assistance of undergraduate sociology majors at Emmanuel College.) The median age was found to be 46. Half the sample was selected from above and half from below this limit. To get the parish strata all the parishes of the diocese had to be classified. This necessitated a survey of the parishes and a classification by parish types. In the end, each parish was classified into one of the following categories:

1. Central urban and transient (in-town parishes)
2. Central urban in medium-sized city or large town
3. Central urban national parish, that is, having an ethnic group
4. Old suburb close to the city
5. Working-class section of small or medium-sized town
6. Small, old town with no suburban influx
7. Suburban influx mixed with old residential area of small or medium-sized town
8. New suburb growing, mostly middle-class professional people with some skilled-worker families
9. Exclusive suburb or small town, new or old (class factors)
10. Resort town—vacation parish

Parishes were coded according to the agreement of three independent judges familiar with the diocese. For selecting the sample, the first five groups were classified as urban and the other five as suburban. From this division it was found that 231 parishes were classified as urban and 160 as suburban. After the parishes were classified, each priest on the diocesan list was coded as type A, B, C, or D. Type A meant under forty-six years and in an urban parish; B, forty-six years or over and in an urban parish; C, forty-six years or over and in a suburban parish; D, under forty-six years and suburban. These four divisions produced age and geographical strata. Within each of these strata, a random sample was chosen. Special thanks is due to Monsignor William J. Daly and Monsignor John A. York for assisting with this complex survey.

[9] David Wallace, "A Case for and against Mailed Questionnaires," *Public Opinion Quarterly*, XVIII, No. 1 (1954), 40-52.

problems loomed particularly large in this case because of the nature of the study and the prospective sample. Since one of the hypotheses questioned the commitment of some clergy to modern research methods, use of the mail seemed doubly precarious. There were distinct advantages, however, such as simultaneity, anonymity, the opportunity to fill in the responses at leisure, and freedom from interaction with an interviewer. These were elements needed to insure spontaneity of response to the orientation items and sincerity in the personal information section. In the light of these advantages a search was made for methods to maximize returns and accuracy of content. To assure maximal return a cover letter carefully explained the general purpose and importance of the research and the necessity of personal cooperation for its success. The questionnaire was arranged to look as short as possible with clear and easily marked recording space. A self-addressed stamped envelope encouraged immediate return. After three weeks a personalized follow-up letter to nonrespondents was mailed with another copy of the questionnaire. Another follow-up letter was sent five weeks later reporting the number of returns already in. This included a return postcard with a checklist to explain the reason for nonreturn and a request for another questionnaire if it was needed.[10] As a result a 70 per cent response was completed within two and a half months. Table 4.1 reports the distribution of the sample contacted and the returns received. A study of the per cent of respondents reveals that the younger suburban group and the older urban group are equally represented in the returns (25 per cent each), and the younger urban group with 29 per cent is overpresent, whereas the older suburban group has the smallest representation (21 per cent). What the table does not report is the way this distribution relates to the number contacted. Of the older urban men 62 per cent returned their questionnaire forms, while 74 per cent of the older suburban men did so. In the younger group 72 per cent of the urban and 74 per cent of the suburban forms were returned. This means that a much larger number (103 as compared with 82) had to be sent to the city

[10] See Sol Levine and Gerard Gordon, "Maximizing Returns on Mail Questionnaires," *Public Opinion Quarterly*, XXII, No. 4 (1958), 569-75 for reasons why all these arrangements assure more responses.

pastors who are older, to get the same returns as from the suburban younger men.

Of the 367 men to whom questionnaires were sent, 259 or 70 per cent responded by returning the form filled out as requested. (Only 2 per cent of all items on the orientation scale were not answered. A much larger number failed to fill in parts of the background data.) Reports on 20 others explained why they failed to respond. Six were too ill; two could not speak sufficient English. Three priests pleaded the mounting pressure from work; and four insufficient experience. Three priests had died. Two others used substitute respondents, and therefore their forms could not be used. This leaves 85 others unaccounted for. Of these, 54 per cent were under 46. Within this group

table 4.1

SAMPLE CONTACTED AND RESPONDENTS BY AGE AND TYPE OF PARISH

Parish Type	Sample Contacted						Number of Respondents					
	Age						Age					
	Under 46		46 or Older		Total		Under 46		46 or Older		Total	
	N	%	N	%	N	%	N	%	N	%	N	%
Urban	106	29	103a	28	209	57	75	29	64	25	139	54
Suburban	82	22	76	21	158	43	64	25	56	21	120	46
Total	188	51	179	49	367	100	139	54	120	46	259	100

a *The slight variations from equal sets are due to corrected categorizations after census data revealed errors.*

54 per cent were from the city. The other 46 per cent, who were forty-six years or over in age, included 64 per cent from city parishes and only 34 per cent from the suburbs. The entire group of nonrespondents represented one-fourth of each stratum in the sample except for the older suburban group, which had the fewest nonrespondents, only 18 per cent. The percentage of pastors who did not respond is almost exactly the same as for those who did, while that of curates was just 4 per cent more than the per cent in the returned sample, 67 per cent. Thinking that ethnicity might make a difference, family names of nonrespondents were examined, and 70 per cent of these were found

to be Irish. This was almost the same percentage that respondents yielded, and here we have exact information. From this evidence one may conclude that nonrespondents possess social characteristics similar to those of respondents. Reports of a more informal nature indicated that among nonrespondents, there was a substantial number who disparage questionnaires, but many who filled them out share a similar attitude. From the information available, then, it would appear that as far as age and status are concerned, the nonrespondents were distributed in the diocese in quite the same way as those who answered and that the groups do not differ to any great extent in ethnicity.

PROFILE OF THE DIOCESAN CLERGY

In order to find out what personal and social characteristics were related to scores on the orientations to change, values, and interests, a number of questions were asked concerning childhood and current experiences. (Those factors which were related to the attitude measures will be discussed after the profile is presented in order to clarify which background elements are related to orientation measures, and which others, though plausibly relevant, are in fact unrelated.)

Family and Early Childhood Factors

Over 95 per cent of these priests were born in Massachusetts. Only four were born in a foreign country, three in Ireland and one in France. None of them lived his childhood on a farm, and only 7 per cent in a small town. Half the remainder were brought up in small cities; the rest were reared in large cities. Over half of them while growing up lived in central city parishes, and 23 per cent more in old suburban parishes near the city. National origin statistics revealed that 31 per cent of their parents were not born in America; another 52 per cent were mixed first or second generation on both sides; and 12 per cent were third generation. Real old-stock American, beyond three generations, included only 5 per cent. The largest ethnic group was of Irish origin; 66 per cent of the fathers and 74 per cent of the mothers fell into this category. The next largest group was Italian, but it constituted only 7 per cent. Parental religion statistics revealed that 98 per cent of the mothers and 94 per cent of the fathers were

Catholic; 5 per cent of the fathers were Protestant and none Jewish. The parental-educational level ranged from about 61 per cent who had attained eighth grade or less, to 3 per cent of the fathers with masters' or professional degrees. There was only one doctorate among the fathers and three masters' degrees among the mothers. Professionally the largest group of fathers, 21 per cent, were proprietors and managers, 5 per cent were professional men, mostly doctors and lawyers. The second largest group, 20 per cent, were skilled workers. Twelve per cent were in clerical work or sales. Eleven per cent were in protective or service work. Unskilled workers constituted 10 per cent. There were no farmer-fathers.

This distribution indicates that most of these priests came from middle-class families. In response, however, to the question on classification of family social position in their community while they were growing up, 28 per cent placed themselves in the middle class and 67 per cent in the working class. No one claimed the upper class and 2 per cent said lower class.

Within the family group, the following features emerged. Five per cent were the only children in the family, 58 per cent came from families of two to four children and 32 per cent from families of five to eight children, while 2 per cent came from families of nine or more children. Thus most of the priests grew up amid much sibling interaction.

In answer to the question, "In your home did your mother or father make the major decisions?" 31 per cent felt that their parents shared this job equally. Twenty-six per cent assigned the decision-making role to father and 29 per cent to mother. On the question, "Would you say you were closer to your mother or to your father while you were growing up?" 5 per cent chose their fathers; 44 per cent their mothers; 49 per cent claimed they were equally close to both; and only 2 per cent did not respond.

Moving outside the family again to the neighborhood, the statistics show that 42 per cent were brought up in neighborhoods predominantly Irish; 2 per cent Italian; 4 per cent French-Canadian. Only 2 per cent lived in neighborhoods that had a Negro population; 10 per cent had a mixture of Irish and Old American in their childhood neighborhood; while 13 per cent had Irish, French-Canadian, and

Italian subgroups living symbiotically. Forty-two per cent lived in neighborhoods almost totally Catholic, 8 per cent had some Protestant neighbors, and 12 per cent lived in neighborhoods with a scattering of different religious groups.

Education

At grammar school age, 45 per cent attended parochial schools, 40 per cent public, and 13 per cent spent some time in each. Only 1 per cent attended private schools at this level. High school enrollment figures show a little different distribution: 20 per cent parochial; 24 per cent private Catholic (probably Boston College High School); and 40 per cent public with 5 per cent attending both types during high school years. As for college, 83 per cent had A.B. or B.S. degrees or their equivalent, 7 per cent secured masters' degrees, and 6 per cent had doctors' degrees. Three per cent of these were in sacred science. Boston College ranked first among the colleges attended, accounting for 56 per cent of the priests; Holy Cross was second with only 4 per cent, and St. Anselm's 1 per cent. No other college had even 1 per cent, but several different Catholic colleges accounted for 9 per cent more; 2 per cent attended secular colleges only, while 7 per cent went to both secular and Catholic colleges before getting their degrees. Twenty per cent of the priests attended the seminary only for their first degree. Most of the priests, 66 per cent, had even their first degree in theology or philosophy. The humanities ranked second with 18 per cent, and science was represented by 6 per cent (this included economics, sociology, and psychology). Graduate schools in education were attended by 6 per cent of the priests and social work schools by just one priest. Two had studied medicine and one, law. Eighty-six per cent of the priests prepared for the priesthood in Boston's diocesan seminary, and 3 per cent in Roman seminaries. No other center trained more than two of these priests.

Current Status

Study of the priests' current professional roles indicates that 30 per cent are pastors, 63 per cent curates, 3 per cent are doing diocesan administrative work, and 4 per cent have full-time duties as hospital or prison chaplains. Twelve per cent have the honorary title of monsignor. In their present work, 66 per cent classified their own parishes as urban, ranging from transient city centers, with and without ethnic clusters, to old suburbs near the city. Eight per cent are in old towns not yet feeling the influx of new populations from the city, while 13 per cent are stationed where the middle class is moving out from the city into established towns. Here, where the working class predominates in the new influx, 39 per cent are stationed; 5 per cent are building or have built new parishes in new suburbs. One per cent reside in resort towns and 2 per cent do not live in parish houses.

The majority of these priests, 90 per cent, are active in all kinds of parish work, the regular role of the priest. This includes celebration of daily Mass, administration of the sacraments, direction of spiritual organizations of men and women, convert instruction, counseling and work with youth groups, and preaching. A few have specialized jobs as full-time chaplains for state hospitals, prisons, schools, and convents, and as directors of diocesan services in social work and missionary organizations. Job satisfaction is evidenced by the fact that 75 per cent prefer parish work to any other apostolic kind. Fifteen per cent would prefer a life work concentrated in convert instruction, counseling or teaching, and preaching. Currently only 4 per cent of these priests hold office in any secular organization but 18 per cent hold some office in national or statewide Catholic organizations of religious, cultural, or social service types.

Reading Habits

An extensive survey of the reading habits of the sample reveals in general that reading orientation is conservative rather than liberal.[11] In order to relate liberal and conservative reading preferences to political preference, respondents were asked: "How would you describe your political views?" Twenty per cent described themselves as liberal Democrats, 36 per cent as conservative Democrats, 3 per

[11] A checklist of 66 secular and religious journals was included to survey reading habits. These included newspapers, news reviews, general interest magazines, specialized journals, professional, theological, and philosophical works. These were chosen to represent conservative, eclectic, and liberal treatment of their specific content. A full report of survey results can be found in my unpublished thesis, "Values and Interests in the Process of Social Change," Harvard, June, 1963, Chapter Five.

cent as conservative Republicans, and 8 per cent as liberal Republicans, while 25 per cent claimed no party leanings. These results reflect a typical pattern of the New England urban areas, where, politically, conservatives outnumber the liberally oriented. This general pattern indicates that the receptivity for change in the Boston area is not reinforced by general reading practices. Because the stimuli for change that will be presented in the second part of the study were taken from current periodicals and books, this reading report becomes a critical factor in judging responses.

SOCIAL CORRELATES OF THE ORIENTATION TYPES

When the orientation scores were computed for the entire sample, 91, or 35 per cent, of the priests were found to be value-change oriented; 28, or 11 per cent, interest-change; 55, or 21 per cent, value-nonchange; and 73, or 28 per cent, interest-nonchange. Twelve, or 5 per cent, had so agreed with alternate items that they had zero scores and hence were not classifiable. The high number of VC scores indicates a growing openness to change in the diocese especially since many of these, 69 per cent in fact, were below the median age of forty-six years. The next largest group, the INC set, suggests a strong reactionary element and 71 per cent of these are over forty-six years. The VNC group is spread evenly in the age division, 54 per cent being under forty-six years. It is hard to explain the smallness of the IC group and the fact that the majority of these, 71 per cent, are young. (Possibly the instrument is not making a clear distinction between low VC scores and IC scores.)

Table 4.2 shows that age was strikingly related to the orientation scores, in fact this distribution could not have occurred by chance one time in a thousand as the chi square test measures.[12]

All those life experiences usually related to attitude formation such as: (1) affection relations between parents and children, (2) which parent makes the major decisions in the home, (3) ordinal rank of subject among siblings, (4) number of children in the family, and the like, failed to correlate to any significant degree with the orientation

---

[12] For explanation of use of chi square test see Quinn McNemar, *Psychological Statistics* (New York: John Wiley & Sons, Inc., 1955), pp. 212-42.

table 4.2

RELATION OF AGE TO THE ORIENTATION SCORES[a]

Orientation Scores	Age					
	Under 46		46 and Older		Total	
	N	%	N	%	N	%
VC[b]	63	69	28	31	91	100
IC	20	71	8	29	28	100
VNC	30	54	25	46	55	100
INC	21	29	52	71	73	100
Zero scores	5	42	7	58	12	100
Total	139		120		259	

[a] $\chi^2 = 31.23$, 3 d.f., $p < .001$.
[b] VC = *Value-change*, IC = *Interest-change*, VNC = *Value-nonchange*, INC = *Interest-nonchange*.

scores. Place of childhood experience, political preference, and reading habits alone remained explanatory, with age held constant.

Place of childhood made a difference in type of response, but only for special groups—those living in small cities in contrast to large cities, and those living in ethnic city parishes in contrast to old suburbs near the city. Apparently, living in large cities generates two of these attitudes, VC (51 per cent) and INC (48 per cent); while living in a small city produces more IC (50 per cent) and VNC men (64 per cent). Table 4.3 demonstrates this. This geographic factor shows up again in the distribution by parish types of childhood residence as can be seen in the same table. The transient city population yields practically equal distribution of all four categories. The ethnic parishes in contrast to the old suburb near the city have more value-nonchange men (45 per cent) and the old suburbs more interest-change men (43 per cent). These percentages have to be looked at in contrast to the others since the ethnic parish produces only 18 per cent of the IC group, whereas the old suburb produces only 15 per cent of the VNC group. This constitutes a significant difference.

It seems that IC and VNC positions are historically grounded in the little community and represent power and cultural isolation from broader issues of the larger community or perception of these broader

table 4.3

COMMUNITY SIZE AND PARISH TYPE IN CHILDHOOD NEIGHBORHOOD OF RESPONDENTS BY ORIENTATION SCORE

Orientation Scores	Childhood Neighborhood			Childhood Parish Type			
	Small City (under 100,000)	Large City (over 100,000)	Total[a]	Central City transient pop.	Central City ethnic pop.	Old Suburb near city	Total
	N %	N %	N %	N %	N %	N %	N %
VC	28 31	46 51[b]	74 82	11 12	40 44	21 23	72 79
IC	14 50	8 28	22 78	3 11	5 18	12 43	20 72
VNC	24 44	18 32	42 76	7 13	25 45	8 15	40 78
INC	17 33	35 48	52 81	11 15	29 40	19 26	59 81
O	— —	— —	— —	3 25	4 33	4 33	11 88
Total	83	107	190	35	103	64	202

[a] $\chi^2 = 9.96$; 3 d.f., $p < .02$.
[b] *These percentages do not add to 100 because some categories are not included.*

issues only in terms of what is already experienced in the ethnic community. The VC position seems to be more consciously developed as a response to challenges to one's learned beliefs in the eclectic environment of the metropolis, while in the same environment, INC positions appear to be a protective refuge for personality security in the face of contradictions that cannot be solved. These two types, the VC and the INC, dichotomize on almost every significant measure developed in this study, whereas the other two, even though they reflect quite different orientations, frequently have but a chance distribution on most of the background measures used, except for these ethnic and geographical factors. Community interaction, then, is an important factor generating the orientation types.

Political views are significantly related to orientations when the sample is divided, not into Republicans and Democrats since there are only twenty-six Republicans in the entire sample, but when divided as liberals and conservatives as described in Table 4.4. In contrast to the distribution of liberals and conservatives, having no political preference resulted in a near chance distribution of scores on the orientation measures. Evidently the connotation of liberal and conservative includes more than preference for specific political programs, since it relates so directly to these measures of VC and INC. This is consistent with the findings in the remainder of the study.

The most consistent relationship that holds through several measures is that between the reading of Catholic publications and the orientation scores. Most of the secular reading done by the priests in the diocese is in the more conservative business periodicals. For this reason there is no evidence of a relationship between this reading and the attitude scores, but the case is quite different for the reading of Catholic periodicals. Here the reading of the journals that are open to change and critical of the *status quo* in its orientation to the social apostolate is significantly related to the value-change orientation, whereas not reading in these journals is as highly related to the interest-nonchange position. There is little relation evident to the other two orientations. *America* is read by men of all four orientations, but reading *Commonweal* and *Jubilee* is a VC practice. The more specialized Catholic journals, *Cross Currents, Review of Politics,*

table 4.4

POLITICAL VIEW AND ORIENTATION SCORES

Orientation Scores	Liberal Democrat		Liberal Republican		Conservative Democrat		Conservative Republican		No Party Leaning	
	N	%	N	%	N	%	N	%	N	%
VC	37	40	6	5	26	28	—	—	20	21a
IC	6	21	2	7	12	43	1	4	7	25
VNC	8	15	8	14	23	45	3	5	13	24
INC	10	7	4	5	28	38	3	4	23	32
O	3	25	0	—	8	67	0	—	0	—
Total	64		20		97		7		63	

a *Percentages do not add up to 100 because 77 nonrespondents are excluded.*

and *Social Order,* which deal with social issues specifically, are related to the VC orientation. Among religious journals reading *Theology Digest, Theological Studies,* and *Catholic Biblical Quarterly* is more related to the VC orientation and reading *The Priest* and *The Homiletic and Pastoral Review* more related to INC. Table 4.5 shows that although not many priests read "open" and "critical" theology journals, reading them is significantly related to the VC orientation, whereas this is not true for reading "the traditional and eclectic journals." The same type distribution follows for reading the other sets of journals listed previously.

There is no way of knowing from these results whether people oriented to values and change seek out the journals that reflect their attitude preference or whether their preferences have been developed from reading the journals. The results suggest that although being young increases one's orientation to VC, the older group can retain or acquire this orientation by reading change-oriented Catholic literature. Something in the environment or in the personality generates a questioning attitude toward the basic problems of man in our times. With this desire to understand and to seek the meanings of what is experienced, certain journals which probe the relevant problems come to be sought out more and more by a select group of thinkers, who in

table 4.5

THEOLOGICAL JOURNALS AND ORIENTATION SCORES[a]

Orientation Scores	Open and Critical		Traditional and Eclectic	
	Theology Digest, Theological Studies, Catholic Biblical Quarterly		Priest, Homiletic and Pastoral Review	
	N	%	N	%[b]
VC	29	32	44	48
IC	7	25	15	53
VNC	13	24	36	65
INC	8	11	47	64
Total	57		142	

[a] $\chi^2 = 8.15$; 3 d.f.; $p < .05$.
[b] *Percentages do not add up to 100 because some categories are not represented.*

time come to share a definition of the situation quite different from that represented in the traditional-oriented periodicals. These change-oriented journals included *Commonweal, Jubilee, Cross Currents, Theology Digest, Theological Studies,* and the *Catholic Biblical Quarterly.*

In summary, then, the only factor that distinguishes IC from VNC men is geographical. IC men come more often from old suburbs near the city while VNC men come in larger numbers from central city ethnic parishes; and both these types come more often from smaller cities than from those with populations over 100,000. On the other hand, both VC men and INC men come more often from very large cities. VC and INC men, the two largest groups in the sample, are distinguished by age, by liberal and conservative political preferences respectively, and by the reading of certain religious journals. Few of the other personal and social characteristics are significantly related to the four orientations once age is held constant. Age distinguishes the VC from the INC group at a highly significant level. Beyond the age factor, reading habits and political preference only distinguish the older men as value or interest oriented.

It may well be that other personal and social characteristics not included in this study are related to the orientation measures. One might be tempted to say at this point that possibly the measures themselves are not measuring anything that is related to the real world, that they are only mental constructs artificially generated and reflective of no underlying attitudes in the subjects who filled out this questionnaire. This is a reasonable supposition that can be evaluated by an examination of the responses of high scorers in the four different categories to the stimuli to change presented to them in interviews. This problem will be considered in the next five chapters.

5

experimenting with pressures to change

The foregoing materials have described orientations to value, interest, and change and the relations of these to characteristics of the total sample of respondents. This has permitted the classification of the sample according to the four categories of value-change, interest-change, value-nonchange, and interest-nonchange. The relevance of these to the theoretical problem may now be briefly restated.

In the controversy among sociologists concerning the place of values and interests as explanatory variables in theories of social change, the persistence of alternate theories to explain the same social phenomena suggested that in different situations it may be possible to perceive either value or interest dimensions as dominating the historical process and that focus on certain moments or situations would account for the contradictions in the theories of the conflict and functional schools. This conclusion suggested the usefulness of examining both value and interest dimensions of some situation currently experiencing noticeable pressures toward change to find out just how values and interests function in the process. It called on one instrument that would measure orientation to values and interests and change and another that would measure the responses of key role players to pressures to change. The construction of such instruments necessitated further delimitation of the scope of the research and the choice of one among many possible approaches to the problem. The approach chosen focuses on behavior at the role level. Examination at this microscopic level runs counter to that approach which perceives broad historical trends in more abstract terms. It is the function of the second instrument to demonstrate how, at this level, the historical trend is set in one direction rather than another. It suggests that the key content of history is revealed in units of choice-making in situations where choices are made in small groups by specific individuals responding to social stimuli of some sort. This instrument was an interview schedule containing a series of stimulus statements urging change in the five areas of interpersonal relations discussed in Chapter Two.

THE INTERVIEW SAMPLE

The sample of respondents for this critical test of hypotheses about how stimuli to change are received by key role players was not the entire group of questionnaire answerers but rather the top ten scorers in each of the four categories of VC, IC, VNC, INC. These men were visited in their parishes and their responses taped. Later these tapes were transcribed and coded. The analysis and interpretations were derived from the coded material. Actually twelve men were interviewed in each category. When the interviewing was almost fin-

table 5.1

ORIENTATION SCORES OF INTERVIEW SAMPLE RANKED FROM HIGHEST TO LOWEST ON VALUE OR INTEREST

Value-change	Value-nonchange	Interest-change	Interest-nonchange
V C	V NC	I C	I NC
85-84	38- 2	24-16	23-38
58-63	38- 2	20-35	22-38
50-50	34-11	22- 7	21-35
44-49	30- 9	19- 1	20-20
43-41	27-44	17-23	18-20
41-38	26-32	17- 4	17-32
37-56	25-21	13-20	17-23
31-35	24- 3	13-16	16-36
30-47	14-26	13-12	16-22
27-27	3-28	12- 6	15-39

ished, however, the IBM 7090 program which was checking the hand-coded questionnaires revealed that a grave error had been made in the original scoring. Fifty of these were recorded incorrectly. This meant that thirteen of those interviewed did not have scores that warranted an interview. Because the time and cost involved would not allow further interviewing, the set for analysis was reduced to ten of each type, and the "extra" interviews were used for testing coding categories.

A central problem of selection was the determination of what constituted a high score. In ranking, one must choose between the value-interest dimension and the change-nonchange dimension, for the same man can be high on one and low on the other. For this study a high value or interest score was taken as the major dimension, since the theoretical problem relates directly to this measure. A compromise was made whenever several men close in rank on value or interest had very low change or nonchange scores. In this case some of these were skipped and lower ranking men with much higher change and nonchange scores were taken.[1] Table 5.1 reports the scores of the sample interviewed. Here it can be seen that the IC scores are quite low on change and the VNC scores are most variable.

Not until all decisions had been made concerning who would be included in the sample by score were the respondents' code numbers matched with their names to find out who was to be contacted. The identification of these respondents was a revealing experience. There are in the entire sample of 259 men only 9 who have charge of special diocesan programs; yet 8 of these 9 are in the interview sample because of their high scores. Pastors and monsignors were also overselected. Table 5.2 describes the distribution of respondents by clerical role. Diocesan specialists are predominantly VC men and pastors INC men. Value-nonchange men are found in all roles but IC men are predominantly curates. The IC distribution is not in line with the expectations set up in the paradigm in Chapter One. This will be considered when the interview results are analyzed. Table 5.3, which

---

[1] The tenth man in the VNC set is not next in rank. He was one of the respondents interviewed by mistake and was included here because his score, though low, was in the right category, and because, although I was lacking one subject, there was no more time for interviewing—an unfortunate but necessary compromise.

gives the age distribution in the four categories, is interesting just from its internal consistency. It suggests that a value orientation is not determined by age but that an interest orientation may suffer a reversal in time shifting a man from a change to a nonchange preference.

CONTACTING THE SAMPLE

In response to a letter asking permission to interview, there were only two refusals, one VC man and one INC man. Summer proved an excellent time for interviewing since the priest at home was on duty and sure to be available at the time agreed upon. A nun-

table 5.2

INTERVIEW SAMPLE BY ORIENTATION SCORE AND CLERICAL ROLE

	Value		Interest	
Change	Administrators	5	Administrators	0
	Pastors	2	Pastors	1
	Curates	3	Curates	9
Nonchange	Administrators	2	Administrators	1
	Pastors	4	Pastors	7
	Curates	4	Curates	2

table 5.3

INTERVIEW SAMPLE BY ORIENTATION SCORE AND AGE

	Value		Interest	
Change	Over 46	5	Over 46	2
	Under 46	5	Under 46	8
Nonchange	Over 46	5	Over 46	8
	Under 46	5	Under 46	2

interviewer turned out to be an appropriate innovation fitting into the change-oriented character of the entire interview. All categories of respondents were able to assimilate this role and no overt hostility appeared in the 52 respondents interviewed.

Most of the interviews took place in the reception room at the local rectory. The first moments on arrival were spent looking for an electric outlet for the tape recorder. This diversion usually generated an informality that made the introduction relatively relaxing. Only in a few instances did a cold formality characterize the experience. In a number of instances the content of the schedule elicited a growing enthusiasm and interest. In a few it caused withdrawal and reserve.

THE INTERVIEW SCHEDULE

The schedule for the interviews was carefully prepared to simulate a normal life experience in which the respondent is faced directly with criticisms constituting pressures to change and asked to express his reaction to them. The content covered the five areas discussed earlier: (1) command-obedience relations; (2) social responsibility; (3) independence training for children; (4) respect for the intellectual life; (5) motivational awareness. Each section of the schedule emphasized one of these and consisted of quotations from the works of change-oriented theologians, philosophers, social scientists, and men of letters in the Church exhorting fellow Catholics to initiate, or at least to cooperate with, those types of change they believe are urgently needed. These quotations were chosen not on the assumption that the unique statements of these men constituted the initial pressure to change, but that statements of this type are currently being expressed by many in the Church because of existing need for change in these areas.[2] The authors were not identified in the interview lest their status constitute in its own right, a pressure to agree or disagree.

[2] Evidence from a popular source written two years after these questions were selected reinforces the fact that these quotations represent pressures to change a direction not currently institutionalized in the Church. An article in *The New Yorker* reporting on the opening of the Second Vatican Council from Rome in October of 1962 observed: "Though, in all, some eight hundred bishops and theologians from every corner of the world were brought to Rome for consultation regarding this agenda, certain outstanding Catholic figures were excluded, or only invited as consultors toward the very end of the preparatory period. Among those excluded or invited late were the American Jesuits John Courtney Murray and John L. McKenzie; the French theologians Henri deLubac, M. D. Chenu, and Jean Daniélou; and Hugo and Karl Rahner of Innsbruck. These men are apparently considered to hold wildly liberal views, and therefore to be dangerous." Xavier Rynne, "Letter from Vatican City," *The New Yorker*, October 20, 1962, p. 102.

Each of the five sections of the interview schedule included an introduction, a set of four quoted criticisms, and a series of questions to probe further into the implications of the quotations. The introductions defined the current situation as needing change and set the theme for subsequent statements. The questions were deliberately worded to project the respondent back into the social milieu in which these pressures would normally arise. The intention was to make the interview experience, as far as possible, a recognizable link in the historical process. It was hoped that the interview would elicit the same kind of responses that would be evoked if a fellow priest, a parishioner, or any member of the secular community made such a suggestion for change at this level of generality. In other words, the instrument was expected to pick up the respondents' spontaneous and public response to pressures to change. The expectation was that people have characteristic ways of responding which either encourage or discourage those urging change to seek further cooperation from them and which cue others to the value or interest direction of the respondents' orientation to the change pressure.

Wherever the quotations or questions took a position on the value-interest dimension, the position taken was always for value. Although this limited the information the instrument could gather, it was done intentionally. In a real life situation the person pressuring for change cannot be both interest and value oriented at the same time. All that can be studied by one interviewer trying to be part of the historical process is response to pressures stemming from one of these orientations. If, as is hypothesized here, people tend to emphasize one orientation rather than the other in their spontaneous, nonexperimental behaviors, any combination would make the situation artificial. In summary then, this was an instrument made up of value-oriented stimuli to change, so presented as to be perceived as part of the historical process in a limited sense, and administered to a sample of priests known for their orientations to change, values, and interests. These orientations had been measured by the mailed questionnaires returned from one to six months prior to the interview in which the second instrument was used. The content of the interview schedule in its five separate parts follows.

Change Pressures: Command-Obedience Relations

As an opening item each respondent was asked to discuss changes concerning command-obedience relations. This was introduced by observing:

There are some in the Church who feel that currently the Catholic community is faced with problems of authority both in the form of oversubmission and irresponsible disobedience. I mean a condition of uncritical submission to arbitrary demands for obedience along with irresponsible rebellion against legitimate demands. . . . Father, do you meet problems of this kind in your work?

If the respondent answered "Yes," he was asked how he explained them to himself. If his answer was "No," then he was asked why he thought criticisms like this were made. These two questions were repeated several times in the interview to discover the respondents' degree of awareness of the type of criticism being discussed and his willingness to state his own position in value or interest terms.

The four quotations in this section dealt directly with authority relations.

(1) The first one was intended to be rather diffuse, with succeeding ones becoming more pertinent to the issue. "At times one would think the only virtue in the Church is obedience."[3]

This quotation merely poses the centrality of the obedience concern. It was introduced with these words: "Suppose a fellow priest made this statement to you." It was followed by this question, "How would you respond to him?" Always an agreement or disagreement was asked for and then a reason for it. If the question was interpreted in such a way as to avoid meeting the real issue of obedience, a further question was asked, "Do you ever worry about command-obedience, or authority relations as a problem in the Church?" followed by a "Why?" or a "Why not?" By asking "Why" or "Why not?" it was hoped that the respondent would express characteristic ways of defining the situation, with certain styles of response, defenses, and pat-

[3] Yves Congar, *Lay People in the Church*, trans. D. Attwater (Westminster, Md.: Newman Press, 1957). The substance of this reference is on page 147.

terns of accepting or rejecting the ideas presented. Later, these could be classified and studied to see if, within each group, there was any consistency in the use of certain types of response to pressures to change.

(2) The second quotation was a little more insistent:

> Modern youth reserve faith for divine truth; they want human procedures explained to them intellectually so that they can judge and criticize. That sense of faith our ancestors had, which permitted the young to make an act of faith in the intellectual or spiritual training he or she was receiving, no longer prevails.[4]

It dealt with changing attitudes toward accepting direction. If the respondent agreed with this statement, he was then asked: "Is this a healthy trend or one of the evils of our day?" Confronted with this direct question, the respondent found it hard to evade. Actually a few did manage to dodge or to take another position, but for the most part the respondents began, at this point, to take a position for or against what was being defined.

(3) The third statement explicitly criticized:

> This conference gives to American Catholics a solemn warning that whoever is responsible, the image of the Catholic Church which has been created in the American minds is not the image of the Church of Christ. It is largely an image of a power structure. I remind you gentlemen, that bricks are not made without straw, and part of this responsibility, a heavy part, rests with Catholics themselves.[5]

Here the respondent is asked if he is aware of the image of the Church as a power structure. To discover differences in perception of how the Church is seen from outside, this quotation was followed by a question: "Do you think that the majority of non-Catholics opposed to public activity of the Church in the community have this view of the Church?" A further question was added to be sure that the meaning was clear. "Have you ever heard the Church called fascist?" If

---

[4] Robert W. Gleason, S.J., *To Live Is Christ: Nature and Grace in the Religious Life* (New York: Sheed & Ward, 1961), adapted from p. 44.

[5] Quoted by John Cogley, "Is the Church a Power Structure?" *Information*, August, 1959, p. 17. The quotation varies slightly from this source because it was taken originally from a newspaper report.

"Yes" was the answer here, then the respondent was asked why he thought the epithet was used. This question could reveal how much information was contained in an opinion, and it could also generate a projection. It did both.

(4) The last quotation in this section underscored the problem that is most pressing in Church command-obedience relations.

> There is much that needs doing to cure lay people of their mania for looking for direction that dispenses them from thinking out their own problems and to dissuade the clergy from their habit of deciding and prescribing everything.[6]

Clergy-laity relation is explicitly the concern here. After asking for an agreement or disagreement with comments, the next problem was presented to bring the issue right to the local situation with the question: "If a movement developed in this archdiocese to consider really serious changes in clergy-laity relations and you had an opportunity to initiate some action, would you accept it?" The responses which yielded a variety of reactions will be analyzed in the following chapters.

Change Pressure: Social Responsibility

The introduction to the second section was somewhat didactic, stating that, "There is great stress today on the idea of personal responsibility for our own decisions and social responsibility for the kind of society we live in." This was followed by the question: "Do you think there are pressing problems today that indicate that Catholics have not in fact taken their share of responsibility for making the community reflect the principles of Christian ethics?" The four quotations were again ordered to lead to a realization of the acute need for change.

(1) The first one introduces a comparative element:

> Charity to be effective today must express itself in human terms. It must take part in revolutionary action against a world in which economic institutions and political injustices condemn a large part of mankind to a life of misery. The first cause of this state of things is the faulty division of wealth which the Popes have often condemned. Against this

[6] Congar, *Lay People in the Church*, p. 417.

social injustice men have risen from every class. But it must be acknowl-
edged that most of these men belong to the non-Christian world and that
Christians too often have supported and now support a set-up which
benefits them, without troubling themselves to examine whether these
conditions are a violation of justice and consequently whether they are
contrary to God's law.[7]

The developing concern with issues of social justice pointed up by the
growth of Communism is the concern here. If this statement was
evaded or if the respondent only addressed himself to the latter part
of it, taking exception to the comparison with the non-Christian
world, then a further question was asked: "If you look at conditions
today in South Africa, the Belgian Congo, South America and India,
as well as in our own South and in our city slum areas, are you satisfied
with the way Christians have dealt with the problems of the community in these areas?" Lest anyone should have failed to make the
transition from the failure of Christians to the rise of Communism,
the next question posed this problem explicitly: "There are some
who can trace the roots of atheistic Communism to a deep resentment
against the Christian world because of its failure to handle the social
problems of the countries where it flourished in the nineteenth century." Then the subject was asked: "Do you usually associate the rise
of Communism with the failure of Christians to attend to the problems of social justice in their community?" If the link was still not
made, a further question was then asked: "Why is it that the Communist Party has been more successful in predominantly Catholic
countries than in countries that are specifically Protestant?"[8]

(2) The second statement focused on the local level:

We tend to stand up and play our full role as citizens only when
we as a group are in some way being threatened. . . . I think we should
all give serious thought to the proposition that Catholic separatism is no
longer justified. It is wasteful, irresponsible, self-defeating. I am ready to

---

[7] Jean Daniélou, *The Christian Today*, trans. Kathryn Sullivan (New
York: Desclee, 1960), pp. 34-35.

[8] From Louis J. Twomey, S.J., "Is Catholic Education Meeting the Challenge of the Modern Crisis?" *College Newsletter*, XXIV, No. 2 (1961), 1, 6-10.
This is the official organ of the College and University Department of the National Catholic Educational Association.

recommend a total reorientation of Catholic teaching about our obligation to the liberal society in which we live.[9]

The question of Catholics distributing charitable services and other
welfare benefits only among Catholics or with preference for Catholics is condemned in this criticism of separatism. This was followed
by questions about the separatism of Catholic organizations of vet-
erans, labor guilds, girl scouts, and, finally, Catholic schools. For the
latter the question was, "Do you think that as they are now con-
ducted, Catholic schools tend to be divisive in that those who graduate
from them are concerned with the Catholic community but not with
the community as a whole?"

(3) A sentence from Cardinal Suhard's 1946 Pastoral Letter to the
diocese of Paris was quoted next:

It is impossible to be a saint and live the gospel we preach without spending ourselves in a common effort to provide everyone with housing, employment, food, leisure and education necessary for a decent
human life.[10]

Here the relation of social justice to sanctity is presented. The question following this statement was one of the most incisive in the entire
schedule. Apparently it was appropriately placed to elicit a spontaneous response. The question was this: "If you were called upon by a
civic committee to join in a Fair Housing Practice effort to get a
Negro family placed in a good home in your parish, a home they could
afford but because of restrictive covenants had not been able to
purchase through real estate agents, what would you do?" No question better demonstrated that there were tremendous differences
among the orientation groups in their awareness of and feeling for
the existence of real problems for Negroes in American cities today.
The responses to this question will be discussed in detail in Chapter
Nine.

(4) The last quote called for critical re-evaluation of methods of
living the gospel:

[9] John Cogley in an address to the graduates of St. John's College,
Minnesota; reported in *America*, July 4, 1959, p. 495.
[10] Emmanuel Cardinal Suhard, *Growth or Decline? The Church Today*,
trans. James Corbett (South Bend, Ind.: Fides Publishers, 1948), p. 87.

The Catholic Church in America was never inflicted with a greater handicap than the "Jesus and I" concept of religion which was taught for so many years in our parochial schools, and which has done so great harm to the formation of apostolic Catholic Americans. . . .

On the basis of this criterion, I question very strongly whether the average Catholic has any sense of mission which he must have to be a full Catholic. I question whether the average Catholic ever contemplates the human race from the tenets of his religion or understands his religious obligations toward his fellowman as an individual and a collective totality.

The sad fact of the matter is that many unbelievers often have a more alert sense of responsibility than a majority of Catholics both cleric and lay. How rarely we find a Catholic who can identify himself with the Cuban peasant or the Japanese coal miner or the Indian untouchable. Karl Marx for all his errors, had this sense of oneness.[11]

Social responsibility is here equated with the Catholic way of life. Then followed the question, "Do you think it is true that the average Catholic as a result of the training we have given him is more concerned with individual sanctification than with deep concern for the welfare of the peoples of the world?" For many this was the high point of the interview. For some it was a confirmation of what they had been thinking right along; for others it offered a possible solution for the many problems previously raised and to which they had not given close attention before or for which they could find no answers. Several VNC men, reluctant at first to be interviewed, became warm and responsive at this point. This was something of a confirmation of the original description of this group as not committed to resisting change as a value but resistant to change simply because they have assumed the social system was blessed in its present form. If this were proved otherwise to them, they would then be open to change.

Change Pressure: Independence Training for Children

This section dealt with forms of youth training in all kinds of organizations. Where negative responses were used it is hard to know whether they were due to rejections of the stimulus or to resistance, since this area, independence training for children, is one in

[11] Albert J. Nevins, "Personalism Stifling Apostolic Spirit," *World Campus,* IV (November, 1960), 1.

which the level of awareness of what constitutes the problems was not high even where the problem was recognized as real. The introduction focused the pressure on a current issue:

> For life in a democracy wherein each man has important choices to make that will affect the lives of many others—it is frequently stressed that independence training, or training to take responsibility, to initiate action, to accept criticism for one's failures and to respond with more creative effort is crucial for the effective functioning of the system.

The question that followed asked if they were satisfied with the training methods used in Catholic schools and parish societies for the young. Many of these priests had charge of youth groups, but for the most part instead of referring to their own groups they applied the question to the schools and therefore claimed little experience in this area.

(1) The four pressures to change again had a sequence of increasing intensity. The first item was a cartoon which far from pressuring to change taught a lesson of "blind" obedience for children in the teacher-pupil relation.[12] It actually posed a dilemma because it juxtaposed child initiative with disobedience to a precautionary command. The respondents were not asked to evaluate the behaviors of the children in the cartoon (though some did this), but rather, they were asked if they thought our children today should be taught this kind of lesson. The question sought to measure an awareness of the problems of discipline facing trainers of children today. Although the answers revealed a wide range of differences in insights about training to initiative and responsibility, this question was added to get a more complete statement of their position on training children: "In the training of children what do you think is the most important thing to teach considering the times in which we live?" This allowed for a wide range of expression of pet theories and of clichés like "obedience and respect for authority." Both kinds of response were made.

(2) The introduction to the next statement differed from the others in that the speaker was identified as a "brilliant young woman who has since left the Church."[13]

---

12 Reproduced by permission of the author.

13 Inclusion of this stimulus can be criticized as not parallel to the others since it was made by someone who "has since left the Church," whereas

INDEPENDENCE TRAINING: FIRST ITEM.

LITTLE BEEP *KNOWS WHAT HELPS MOST*

ITEM: DO YOU THINK THIS IS THE KIND OF LESSON OUR CHILDREN NEED TODAY?

It is not facts the Catholic students are lacking: it's the critical attitude. And I'm forced to the conclusion that their intellectual plodding and timidity has been bred into them by their schooling; I say this because the few Catholics that I know who are intellectually daring and come from Catholic colleges invariably had persistent and continual trouble with the administration and their teachers. [Private correspondence]

The pressure here is to look not only at the effect of dependency training but also at hostile reaction to the use of initiative in a dependency-oriented system. Projection was expected from some respondents who would reject the content because of their rejection of the speaker for her defection. Respondents were asked if they thought the criticism was totally unjustifiable, justified in part, or quite justified. If they thought the statement justified, they were asked why they thought so; if unjustified, why they thought the statement had been made.

---

the others were made by "people in the Church pressuring for change." But the statement was originally made when the person was in the Church and pressuring for change, so this criticism does not hold.

(3) The next stimulus observes that Catholic scholarship shows "a lack of industry and the habit of work."[14] This points to an effect of dependency training. They were asked further if they considered Catholics less oriented to work than other Christian or non-Christian groups.

(4) Ending the third section was a quotation speaking of the Church in Ireland:

> The Church taken in this broad sense as a social institution offers, in the opinion of many, the most acute expression of the tendency to treat the general public as too immature to make its own decisions.[15]

Here, finally, the Church is implicated to some extent in the existence of the problem. The question that followed was: "Do you think there is any tendency for Catholic educators in the parish and parochial school to assume and hence to reinforce an immaturity in those they instruct?" A further question was, "Why do Catholics choose secure jobs like civil service, police and fire department work?"

When one considers the extensive literature written by social scientists about Catholic attitudes toward work, stemming from the "Protestant Ethic" analysis of Weber,[16] the responses to this question by men active in the life of the Church revealed surprisingly little awareness of this negative evaluation of Catholic performance in the area of work. For the most part they had not heard these criticisms, or if they had heard them, they had not considered them as having any basis in reality.

Change Pressure: Respect for the Intellectual Life

The introduction referred to the flood of self-criticism of Catholic scholarship precipitated in 1955 with Monsignor John Tracy Ellis' critique of Catholic performance in scientific, technological, and general intellectual life. It added: "He and other critics found Catholics still prone to expect immediate divine intervention rather than

---

[14] John Tracy Ellis, "American Catholics and the Intellectual Life," *Thought*, XXX, No. 3, (1955), 375.

[15] Gary McEoin, "Ireland: Vacuum of National Purpose," *America*, November 14, 1959, p. 185.

[16] See Max Weber, *The Protestant Ethic and the Spirit of Capitalism*, trans. Talcott Parsons (London: George Allen & Unwin, 1930). See also *Sociological Analysis* XXV, No. 1 (1964), entire issue.

that God would expect us to use our intellects and wills to work on modern problems and create the world of the future."

(1) The first quoted criticism stated:

> In their justified contempt for the apologetic use of science there are scholars who come to despair of the Church. No doubt the clergy could be better prepared than it now is to grasp the requirements of or even the relevance of scholarship.[17]

This expression of annoyance at a perceived common clergy attitude toward serious learning was taken from an article on the intellectual and spiritual life. The question that followed, however, was too easy to evade. It read: "Do you think the clergy for the most part today show genuine respect for scholarship or do you think there is some truth in this criticism?" A further question asked if they thought the criticism relevant enough to warrant changes in the present curriculum of seminaries and Catholic schools. There was some general resistance in responding to this. In some cases this was due to a genuine feeling of inadequacy to handle directly such an explicit problem. The question was asked to find out who had been working on this problem sufficiently to have gathered specific ideas for change.

(2) The next quotation pushed the criticism further:

> We run into the astonishing fact that Catholic education even on the higher levels does not aim at making scholars. It seems satisfied with developing a defiant reaction to modern scholarship.[18]

Here the university is included in the criticism. After this the respondents were asked directly if they found a tendency to anti-intellectualism among priests.

(3) The third statement pressed even further:

> Even today it is rare for Catholics to be at the start of broad intellectual developments. Only when these developments become threats or unavoidable issues do we respond. The very fact that so much of our talk of Catholic intellectualism is couched in the language of "meeting challenge," "countering threats," "taking our place," and so on indicates that initiative and foresight are not our strong points.[19]

[17] George H. Tavard, "The Intellectual and Spiritual Life," *Spiritual Life*, V, No. 3 (1959), 187.

[18] *Ibid.*, pp. 191-92.

[19] Much checking and letter writing has not revealed the original source of this stimulus statement.

Here suggestion gives way to specificity. Church leaders are criticized for being concerned with the intellectual life only for interest-oriented reasons. If this statement was rejected, the respondent was asked how he explained the rash of literature on intellectualism and the Catholic that has been published over the last ten years.

(4) The final statement in this section read: "Churchmen have not pondered enough the case of Galileo."[20] It was a concise judgment of the clergy from a lay source. Respondents were asked if they agreed or disagreed.

There was evident resistance to the third and fourth sections. Some of this was due to content and some to the fact that these priests, because of their training, would consider these problems the concern of the schoolman but not of their parish roles. Still others, involved in the intellectual revival within the Church, were a little impatient with this continued stress on what for them was a problem in the process of being solved. The O'Dea quotation proved an excellent differentiating item between the deniers, evaders, and acceptors and produced various forms of defense, explanation, and clarification.

Change Pressure: Motivational Awareness

Cooperation picked up again in this last section except for a certain few who became progressively more silent. The introductory statement was intended to set the problem in a focus familiar to these respondents, all of whom had been trained in a Thomistic philosophical and theological tradition. It stated:

Because of the tendency of rational psychology to stress the role of the intellect as the human factor in behavior and to downgrade the functions of the emotions as animal, recent emphasis on the role of the unconscious in human behavior has been a controversial issue in some thinking in the Church. This is reflected most popularly in a discussion of the relation of religion and phychiatry, but it has many other ramifications, also.

(1) Without asking for any comment on this statement, the first critical question was introduced:

[20] Thomas E. O'Dea, *American Catholic Dilemma: An Inquiry into the Intellectual Life* (New York: Sheed & Ward, 1958), p. 60.

We are led sadly to suspect that some of the anticommunism in Catholic circles is no more than a form of escapism from the anxieties and frustrations of a harsh and turbulent world.[21]

The respondents were asked if they thought there was any connection between being frustrated and anxious and joining a hate group or any other group that is out to destroy or punish others. This interviewing was done when the John Birch Society was just beginning to receive publicity and when few organizations, Catholic or other, had come out with the now common condemnations of the "radical right." As in the third section, which also handled the psychological aspect more directly, the level of awareness here was not so high as in the political, social, and intellectual areas. In fact, in this section except for the two VC men who had formal psychiatric training, there was no one with a consistent awareness of the functions of the unconscious. The VC man came to respond as had the VNC man in the social justice section, that is, with a sense of discovering information he had been seeking through his unexpressed queries about the why of these pressures. Few expressed understanding of how this section held together. The first question was: "How do you explain to yourself the fact that Hitler's regime actually killed six million Jews?" The then current storm about the Eichmann trial was reflected in some of the responses which ranged from a deep feeling of sharing the guilt to a genuine anti-Semitism. The next one: "Why were many anti-Communists also anti-McCarthyites?" was frequently misinterpreted by those not sharing the definition of the situation that prompted anti-McCarthyism. And finally to the last question: "Why do you think many members of the John Birch Society are Catholic?" the answers ranged from complete unawareness of who Robert Welch was or expressions of enthusiasm for his program, to genuine concern about this "island-of-safety mentality" and about totalitarian methods. These three questions occurring late in a now lengthy interview, received the

[21] "On Fighting Communism," (editorial), *America,* May 22, 1959, p. 269. This quotation was preceded by a descriptive comment relevant to the reasons for its selection. The editor states: "Too often we note this preoccupation [with domestic Communism] is accompanied by coolness toward NATO, by hostility toward foreign aid, by complaints about taxes, by opposition to desegregation, even by defeatist fear of Communist infiltration of Catholic schools and of other Catholic organizations."

enthusiasm of some and in others induced anxiety which continued till the end of the interview.

(2) To investigate the equation of frustration and anti-Communist enthusiasm, the next statement was presented in its original form—an article from the diocesan newspaper, *The Pilot*.[22] The author, Father Bosler, S.J., was necessarily identified, and the respondent was asked if he agreed with the Father's suggestion advising Catholics to stop spending time joining anti-Communist organizations and to get rid of their frustrations by joining the NAACP, the Urban League, and by working for equal employment and housing opportunities for Negroes in their towns. Written as it was, in clever reporting style, and handed to the respondent as a clipping from the paper, it permitted expression of any hostility or genuine concern it may have aroused. Both these responses, as well as indifference, were forthcoming. Right after this, each man was asked if he was familiar with the book called *The Authoritarian Personality*. No one answered "yes."[23]

(3) In the next two quotations, the interview turned just briefly to two other areas of expression of unconscious motivation. The first one repeated the quotation with which the interview opened and added to it what was in the original quotation, namely, "At times one would think that the only virtue in the Church is obedience and the only vice unchastity."[24]

The critical element here is overstress relative to other virtues. The respondents were asked whether in sermons, retreats, and spiritual guidance in general, this vice, unchastity, was not stressed beyond what is needed, in comparison with other vices connected with unkindness, dishonesty, aggression, exploitation, and other forms of social injustice. There was evidence of much more familiarity with this issue and a free expression of opinion followed.

(4) The last statement dealt with prayer:

Many of our modern devotions fail because so often they are wordy, man-centered, devoid of awe and form. They seldom rise to the

[22] May 13, 1961, p. 1.

[23] In the only two cases where there was reason to expect that the respondents might be familiar with this book (that is, the two men having psychiatric training), I neglected to ask the question.

[24] Congar, *Lay People in the Church*, p. 147 for the substance of this statement.

doctrinal level of adult minds. Simply compare the Marian Year Prayer with any of the collects of our missal—a flood of well-meant words drowns the purpose, superlatives are heaped onto each other and every fugitive thought is caught and nailed down in the endless flow. The prayer leaves nothing unsaid and thus deprives the listener of all creativeness: everything is done for us and therefore leaves us numb of spirit. . . . Are we prepared to see that a mind nurtured in great thought must put aside an immature approach to God and to His mystery?[25]

Satisfaction of dependency needs at the very center of spiritual life is considered here. The question was, "Do you think we have currently at the parish level in our spiritual programs a habit of fostering an immature approach to God as referred to here?" Besides evaluating parish programs in general, this question asked for an evaluation of the very center of the priest's own role behavior in the parish. There was a clear differentiation among respondents between those who could agree with this question and those who evaded or rejected it.

A few general questions were added to bring closure less abruptly. One of these proved to be particularly discriminating. It stated: "In general how do you feel about the problems I have raised today?—do they have any relevance to your work?" The responses here were striking. Some were deeply interested while others felt no problems had been raised. Why these and other striking differences in reaction to the same stimuli characterized the respondents will be the subject of the next four chapters.

25 H. A. Reinhold, "The Silence and Singleness of Prayer," *The Current,* II, No. 2 (1961), 63. Adaptation in first and last sentence.

6

**content
analysis:
patterns
of assent
and dissent**

The coding of the interview material taken from the tapes constitutes the critical center of the entire research design. The content analysis of the responses of high scorers in the four orientation groups—VC, IC, VNC, INC—should reveal any patterned or characteristic mode of resistance or acceptance of change that is typically associated with this typology. The central expectations are two: (1) that the responses will be related to the four functional problems of social systems: adaptation, goal attainment, integration, and pattern maintenance, and (2) that they will indicate that these men are making strikingly different choices of action in response to similar stimuli in social situations and are thus affecting the historical process.

In the next four chapters, then, the orientation scores will be taken as the independent variable. Uniformities will be expected within each set to reveal those subtle cues that men read as resistance to or openness to change and to the direction the social process could take. The four different coding instruments will handle (1) patterns of assent and dissent, (2) definitions of the situations, (3) styles of response, and (4) defense mechanisms. Only the first will be treated in this chapter. Chapters Seven, Eight, and Nine will consider the other three.

PATTERNS OF ASSENT AND DISSENT

The agree-disagree continuum was developed from the hypothesis that when ideas about the *status quo* are suggested, a person reveals his position not simply by his "yea-" or "nay-" saying, but by the limits and lengths of his "yes" or "no." This means that the agreement or disagreement by itself communicates little that is important to the future of the situation, but the elaboration, or, in contrast, the lack of it, contains the cues that others interpret and act on when ego responds to a suggestion. For the analysis of patterns of assent and dissent, twelve modes of agreeing and disagreeing were coded. Table

table 6.1

CODING CATEGORIES FOR DETERMINING PATTERNS OF ACCEPTANCE OR REJECTION OF STIMULUS STATEMENTS

1. Respondent accepts the criticism as applicable without distorting the meaning of the statement.
2. Agrees that the criticism was true but is so no longer. Change in the direction urged has already begun or has already taken place.
3. Agrees with the criticism statement but only after changing its meaning.
4. Says "No," he does not accept the criticism, and yet his words indicate that he does.
5. Like number 4, with the added characteristic that he has modified meaning of the statement.
6. Subject neither agrees nor disagrees but clearly specifies some position, for example, "It is normal," or "I agree in part."
7. Subject feels he knows nothing about the matter or too little to comment.
8. Disagrees with the criticism statement but only after changing its meaning.
9. Subject seems to agree but his explanation is a reversal or clearly implies disagreement.
10. Like number 9, with the added characteristic that he has modified the meaning of the statement.
11. Subject rejects the criticism as inapplicable without distorting the meaning of the statement.
12. Answer is an evasion of the question either totally unrelated or so ambivalent that classification into other categories is too problematic.

6.1 describes these. It will be seen that the categories range from the most positive mode of assent to a polar mode of rejection.

Category one was intended to select those people for whom the criticism as stated was part of their real world, who recognized it as a criticism they were ready to accept knowing its implications. It was expected that VC men would be the only ones who could accept most of the statements in the form in which they were presented, since each statement was made in a context that was change oriented and value based. The IC men would be able to accept some of them but not those which they perceived as disadvantageous or without profit for their own groups. Both NC groups should reject most of them, but for the VNC men some of the statements should appeal because of their value component. Thus the widest difference should be between the scores of the VC and INC men. The latter were expected to have the largest scores in category 11 (that is, outright rejection), because the stimulus was change oriented and value based. The IC and VNC men should rank intermediate on agreeing, with the IC group accepting some of the statements, since all were oriented toward change and the value element was not uniformly predominant. Figure 6.1 describes the responses just for categories 1 and 11, that is, straight agreement or straight disagreement.[1]

Figure 6.1 records only straightforward acceptance or rejection of the stimulus statement in its entirety without any elaborations, detractions, evasions, or withdrawals. (See Table 6.1, numbers 1 and 11.) The results are strikingly graduated in the direction expected, the VC men accepting and INC men rejecting.

Categories 6, 12, and 7 from Table 6.1 are related in that they are

[1] There were forty-four items in the interview schedule to which an agree-disagree response could be made. All of these were coded, but only responses to the twenty stimulus statements are included in this analysis. These statements, all chosen from critical works written in the Church since World War II, constitute a consistent stimulus, where some of the other questions following the stimulus statements cannot be so clearly characterized.

The coding was done by two coders working independently after a training period of a week. The first coder was the writer; the other was a graduate student in the Department of Social Relations unfamiliar with the subjects or with the hypotheses. For the entire set the overall coding reliability was .85. For the twenty stimulus statements it was .95. Besides the training period week, the coding itself for this problem alone took 160 coding hours.

forms of avoiding a direct confrontation with the issue. In category 6 the respondent neither agrees nor disagrees but takes another position. As in categories 1 and 11 he apparently sees the issue as real in the form in which it is stated, but he qualifies his answer by such statements as "It is true in some cases but not in others," or "I can agree in part but not with all of it." Category 12, on the other hand, is a real evasion. The respondent may avoid answering the question at all by some remark such as, "Now why would a person make a statement

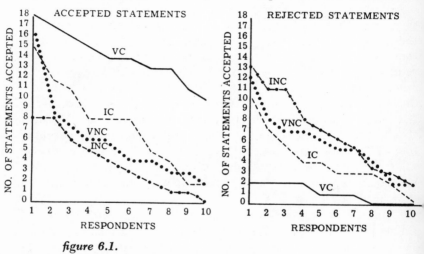

figure 6.1.

THE NUMBER OF STIMULUS STATEMENTS ACCEPTED AND REJECTED BY EACH RESPONDENT (BY ORIENTATION GROUP).

like that; what good will that do?" This expression of annoyance, anxiety, or disparagement makes return to the question difficult. Sometimes at the very outset he may address himself to another question and in this way come to feel that he is doing his part while simultaneously redirecting the conversation. For example, in reply to the statement that some prayers formulated in recent times are too wordy, a respondent answered: "Yes, I agree there is too much public prayer; private prayer is more appealing to my people." This technique of using the responses asked for, but referring them to problems not related to the issue raised, is a common experience in change-oriented situations. It seems to function effectively as a means to resist looking publicly at the problems raised for consideration. Because it can just as well be conscious as unconscious, it is a technique for manipulating a situation as well as an unconscious defense. It is such a common technique that one reads it as a cue to desist. It cannot be classified merely as the defense mechanism of denial even though it may at times fulfill the same function.[2]

THE SIGNIFICANCE OF THE FINDINGS

For a statistical measure of the difference in the rates of types of response that would use all the information available in comparing group with group and that would be more than a comparison of their agree-disagree scores, the coding categories were weighted to form a scale running from acceptance to rejection through all the stages of agreeing, delimiting, not knowing, denying, to complete evasion. This was done by weighting the categories in an order which seemed logically to imply a more extreme form of rejection in each succeeding case. The weights followed the order in which the categories appear in Table 6.1 and equalled the value of each rank.

Category 1 was weighted 1; category 2, 2; 3, 3; and so on up through category 12. Evasion was placed after rejection because refusal even to address oneself to the issue seemed more rejecting than a flat denial of the truth or relevancy of a statement. The ranked responses were then tested to find out if the sums of the ranks revealed a difference great enough to conclude that these respondents could not have been drawn from the same population of assenters and dissenters, by chance. The Mann-Whitney U Test was used.[3] The results were significant beyond the .001 level for the following sets: VC with IC, VC with VNC, VC

---

[2] Roger Walker has demonstrated that people become so skilled in reading intended meanings behind verbal communications that the manifest content of the words used sometimes comes to play only a secondary role in the communication. See Roger Walker, "Communication in a Manufacturing Organization" (unpublished doctoral dissertation, Harvard University, 1961).

[3] For a clear and concise explanation of the Mann-Whitney U Test, see Frederick Mosteller and Robert R. Bush, "Selected Quantitative Techniques," *Handbook of Social Psychology*, Gardiner Murphy, ed. (Cambridge, Mass.: Addison-Wesley Publishing Co., Inc., 1954), I, pp. 316-17.

with INC. But between the IC and VNC, and the VNC and INC, the results could have occurred by chance ten or more times in a hundred. From this it is possible to conclude that the value change men belong to a different population of agreers from the other three groups. What this seems to mean also is that there is a gradation of rejection of change stimuli that is value-based among the four orientation groups in order of VC, IC, VNC, to INC. Both nonchange and interest elicit rejection of these stimuli or at least sufficient ambivalence about them to prevent a spontaneous acceptance. It is, however, possible to determine the presence of pattern even here.

Because it seemed that the style of rejection for the interest group had a character different from that of the VNC group, the same measurement was used again clustering forms of evasion on the one hand and those that were forms of rejection or denial of the truth or relevance of the stimulus on the other. This distinction should separate those who, having examined the stimulus, evaluate it negatively from those who just refuse to look at it or cannot see it at all for some reason not necessarily evident in their responses. For the evasion cluster, categories 6, 7, and 12 were used and weighted in that order. For denial, categories 2, 3, 4, 5, 8, 9, 10, and 11 were weighted in that order. If one is willing to accept the .05 level of significance, then chance is not operating here. The value orientation of the VNC group makes them less likely than the INC oriented to avoid looking at a stimulus to change when that stimulus is grounded in values. This is an interpretation based on the fact that the evasion scale shows that the difference between VNC and INC scores could occur by chance only three times in one hundred. A further inspection of the scores shows that the differences are caused by the higher number of scores in category 12 (evaders) and 7 (those who don't know) for the INC group. Although there is no difference statistically demonstrated by these measures between the IC and VNC groups (a fact that will be recorded a number of times in this study), the source of their scores is different. Where the VNC group uses one-third more evasion (12) than does the IC group, the latter uses twice as much of the "taking another position" (category 6).[4]

---

[4] Because category 6 is weighted less, these differences were reduced in the computation.

CHARACTERISTICS OF EACH ORIENTATION GROUP

Knowing that differences between sets on the agree-disagree scale are significant when scores are weighted within each set by person, we can look at the sums of scores for each category within each set to see what distinguishes each orientation group. Table 6.2 indicates: (1) that VC men have far more straightforward agreements with the stimulus statements than any other group (64 per cent) and that they are less likely than any of the others either to distort the meaning of the statements (3 per cent) or to claim too little knowledge to answer (.9 per cent); (2) that IC men, more than others, avoid the agree-disagree answer and take a third position (12 per cent); (3) that VNC men are most likely to believe that the conditions criticized have already been reformed or are well on the way to such reform (6 per cent); (4) that INC men, besides being the most ready to reject an item unqualifiedly (28 per cent), are also most likely to change the meaning of an item before rejecting it (9 per cent), and to avoid answering it at all (13 per cent).

The question arises whether any one of the areas in which stimuli were presented (that is, command-obedience relations, social responsibility, independence training, respect for the intellectual life, and motivational awareness) received more acceptance or rejection than did others. This is a real issue. When this research was initiated, a hypothesis by Samuel Stouffer proposed that priests would respond differently to the five themes depending on the areas in which they were more involved. He believed that differences by theme would be greater than differences across themes by orientation groups. Thus VC men might be more open to one theme and IC men to another, or all priests irrespective of orientation might resist one theme more than others. Figure 6.2 reveals that his hypothesis is not confirmed and that the main differences in response are due to the amount of agreeing and disagreeing done by the different orientation groups. There is a slight tendency, however, for the INC and the VC groups both to be more open to acceptance of the fifth theme, motivational awareness. All groups except INC are more open to the second theme, social responsibility. Both of these results are in line with the expected self-oriented interests of the INC type. Both value-oriented groups are *table 6.2*

PERCENTAGE OF RESPONSES IN EACH CATEGORY OF THE AGREE-DISAGREE CONTINUUM, BY ORIENTATION GROUP[a]

Category	VC		IC		VNC		INC	
	Per Cent	No. of Responses	Per Cent	No. of Responses	Per Cent	No. of Responses	Per Cent	No. of Responses
1. Accepts criticism	64	281	37	163	27	118	17	79
2. The criticism is no longer a problem	2	10	2	7	6	27	2	8
3. Agrees—with changed meaning	3	13	6	25	5	23	5	23
4. Says disagrees but in discussion agrees	.2	1	.4	2	.9	4	.5	2
5. Same as no. 4 but changes meaning	—	—	—	—	—	—	—	—
6. Takes a third position	9	39	12	51	7	30	8	37
7. Knows too little to comment	.9	4	4	16	3	11	4	16
8. Disagrees—with changed meaning	2	9	2	8	4	16	9	32
9. Says agrees but in discussion disagrees	—	—	—	—	.4	2	.4	2
10. Same as no. 9 but changes meaning	.5	2	.2	1	.5	2	—	—
11. Rejects criticism	6	28	20	90	24	106	28	125
12. Evades question	2	9	12	25	8	34	13	59
13. Question not asked	10	44	12	52	15	67	13	57

[a] $N = 40$; ten respondents in each orientation group. There were forty-four coded items per respondent. This table includes not only the twenty stimulus statements but also every question in the schedule to which an agree or

more reluctant to accept criticism in the area of independence training and respect for the intellectual life. But it is the two nonchange groups that are more prone to use straight rejection of these two themes. Since dependency training is grounded in an old tradition, this is certainly in line with expectations. The VC men do not so readily as expected accept the criticism of dependence training, not because they are rejecting it but because they take a third position or feel that the criticism is no longer applicable. Besides scoring low on social responsibility items, the INC men are also low in acceptance of change in the

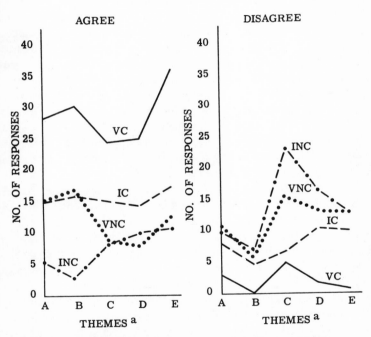

a For the themes, A stands for command-obedience relations; B for social responsibility; C for independence training; D for respect for the intellectual life; and E for motivational awareness.

figure 6.2.

AGREE AND DISAGREE RESPONSES (BY THEME OF STIMULUS STATEMENT).

areas of command-obedience relations. This, too, is in line with the expectations for this group. Submission to "things as they are" would make them reluctant to initiate change in clergy-laity relations, the main content of this theme. Although the differences described in Fig. 6.2 are not significant statistically, they all move in the expected direction.

CONCLUSION

The analysis of the results of using the first coding instrument, the agree-disagree scale, produces substantial evidence that all of the four groups have unique characteristics in the manner in which they accept or reject change-oriented stimuli. (1) The value-changers, as expected, are ready to accept the stimuli to which they are already committed. (2) The interest-change people have the greatest tendency to take a position on the stimulus that commits them neither to accept it nor to reject it as it is presented but to take some considered third position. (3) The value-nonchangers, more than others, recognize the problem but are assured that the remedy is already applied. (4) The interest-nonchangers not only reject the stimulus most often, but, by escaping into the discussion of a related but not pressing problem, are most likely to avoid looking at the issue at all.

Lest it be concluded that this instrument is simply reiterating the findings of the value, interest, change questionnaire and thus only demonstrating that the first instrument really measured differences, it is important to emphasize that the mailed questionnaire did not handle the problems of command-obedience relations, independence training, respect for the intellectual life, or motivational awareness used in the interview. It did mention social justice, which is closely related to the social responsibility section and to all the others indirectly, but it asked only for a show of preference for statements having this label. It did not handle any explicit issues. The patterns in response revealed by this analysis can be caused only by the factors that determined (*a*) the selection of these items, namely, that they are currently related to a value-based pressure to change facing the clergy in the local community and (*b*) the selection of the respondents for their high scores on orientations to value or interest, change or nonchange.

7

content analysis: orientations to the world

Preoccupation with some of the functional problems facing social systems may explain why people in roles tend to view the world in certain characteristic ways. An emphasis on adaptation, goal attainment, integration, or pattern maintenance may be related to resistance to or acceptance of change and the tendency to make choices in value or interest terms. These ideas were developed in Chapter One. It is now time to test them.

Persons concerned with adaptation should perceive the social structure as something that can be changed through new ideas, new division of labor, new ordering of role relations. People concerned with goal attainment should perceive the social system as something that can be manipulated by individuals striving to realize specific goals. On the other hand, if the concern is with integration, then a person's interests should focus on social harmony, order, cooperation, and conformity. The pattern maintenance emphasis should be expressed more in concern for the preservation of style of life valued for its meaning rather than for its form.[1] Thoughts of this type led to the development of a set of coding categories all related to views of the

[1] These expectations focusing as they do on aspects of openness to change and rejection of change are not independent of the orientation scores and hence do not constitute a clear test of the hypothesis of relation of these scores to the four functional categories. On the other hand, the orientations developed from them in the form of views of the world do have a distinct meaning independent of the change-nonchange focus.

world, of social structure, and of people in roles, that might be related to a priest's daily round of duty. All the coding categories had to do with the priest's perception of situational factors. They included perception of (1) the world in general, its size, its relation to the Church, (2) the laity's relation to the clergy, (3) the non-Catholic's relation to the Church, (4) leader-follower relations, (5) expected response to authority, (6) the permanency of social structure, (7) level of sanctity one can expect of ordinary people, (8) the purpose of social action programs, (9) the responsibility of the clergy for conditions in the world, (10) the scope of ethics, (11) the intellectual competence of people in general and of the clergy in particular, (12) the priest's sphere of influence, and others.

Orientations to the world include a broad range of topics, too broad for any one study. The assumption that the definition of the situation is a fundamental determinant of human action and that the functional problems are selective factors in determining how one perceives the world, limited the selection of categories to two main areas: (1) definitions related to social structure and function, and (2) definitions that would be elicited in response to the five themes proposed in the stimulus statements. These still permitted a wide range of choice for categories.

It is important for the understanding of the broader social-psychological issues on which this study is based to recognize that this aspect is a study of perception and, more particularly, of the sociology of knowledge. A man can respond to a situation only as he perceives it, and this perception is limited by the knowledge available to him concerning it.[2] Shared definitions of what is accepted as true or real will immediately make a difference in how stimuli to change are received and interpreted. It has already been shown that pressures to change were denied reality or distorted by respondents in spite of substantial evidence of their reality. It is important, then, to find out if, in the perceptions of social structure, there are basic differences that in some degree account for the variations in response to the stimuli.[3]

[2] See on this point, Gordon Allport, *The Nature of Prejudice*, abridged. (New York: Doubleday, Anchor Books, 1958), Chapter Ten, "The Cognitive Process," pp. 165-77.

[3] On the role of definition of the situation influencing interpersonal behavior, see James G. March and Herbert A. Simon, *Organizations* (New York: John Wiley & Sons, Inc., 1958), pp. 150ff.

It remains to be seen from the codings whether men, interacting in the same situation, tend to perceive it so differently that there is conclusive evidence of selective perception by orientation group. If this should prove to be so, then, since these men are related to each other not in different roles but in similar roles in the system, this study offers a possible explanation of how the individual functions to redirect the social process when he is in a decision-making role—that he acts in terms of a different definition of what is real.

Three problems are being examined here simultaneously: (1) are there essential differences among people in the same role set, in the way they define the social factors related to stimuli to change? (2) are these definitions related to different orientations classified as VC, IC, VNC, and INC? (3) are they grounded in different functional concerns of the social system described as adaptation, goal attainment, integration, and pattern maintenance? First, it is necessary to examine the content of the coding categories and the distribution of respondent scores. Only those categories will be considered that proved reliable after they were coded by two coders working independently.[4] To facilitate this analysis, code themes will be summarized. The themes that subsume all categories are these:

(1) Perception of role relations as taking place between
   (*a*) Peers in the process of upgrading
   (*b*) Elites and masses.
(2) Perception of the source of social order as arising from
   (*a*) Internalized and shared principles or
   (*b*) In the imposition of commands.
(3) Perception of the structure of the social systems as
   (*a*) Capable of being changed by man or as
   (*b*) So permanent that all change occurs in individual behavior only through vague, impersonal forces.
(4) Perception of intergroup relations as open or closed, with
   (*a*) "Open," meaning a lack of emphasis on group boundaries as terminal points for cooperative relations; or
   (*b*) "Closed," meaning an expectation of cooperation within the group and conflict or competition between groups.

[4] The reliability check for this set of categories and the next one, "Styles of Response," was done by the writer and by a coder trained especially for this job.

    (5) Perception of the world
        (*a*) In cosmopolitan or
        (*b*) Local terms.
    (6) Perception of the Church as
        (*a*) A social system sharing the responsibility and hence guilt for present world conditions, or
        (*b*) A closed in-group whose responsibilities and services are limited to a specific localized constituency.

THEME 1—ELITE-MASS VERSUS GENERAL UPGRADING

The elite-mass versus general upgrading theme refers to the contrasting definitions of the structure of modern society that are permeating current literature and social science research.[5] Deriving in a complex way from a number of intellectual and political traditions, the "elite-mass" conception of role relations tends to perceive social structures as power oriented and divided into distinct classes consisting of a mass of subjects and an elite of rulers. The "general upgrading" focus perceives an ever-increasing structuring of peer relations with division by specialization and interdependency, and with functionally specific hierarchies wherein status in one system does not necessarily carry over to another.[6] Table 7.1 gives the categories related to this theme. The idea that there are two kinds of people, two kinds of training, special gifts for some classes, runs through the elite-mass definition of social systems. The idea that, due to economic, educational, and social opportunities open to more people, a new set of role relations is emerging in modern times runs through the "general upgrading" focus. This latter focus assumes that the two-class system is a historical reality belonging to specific social structures but not a general or inevitable characteristic of social structures. Only VC men

[5] See Winston White, *Beyond Conformity* (New York: Free Press of Glencoe, Inc., 1961).

[6] For this "general upgrading" theme see Talcott Parsons and Neil J. Smelser, *Economy and Society, a Study in the Integration of Economic and Social Theory* (New York: Free Press of Glencoe, Inc., 1956), Chapter Five, "The Problems of Growth and Institutional Change in the Economy," pp. 246-94. And for the contrasting elite analysis see C. Wright Mills, *The Power Elite* (New York: Oxford University Press, 1956).

CONTENT OF ELITE-MASS AND GENERAL UPGRADING DEFINITIONS OF THE SITUATION

Theme—Elite-mass and General Upgrading

Definition of the Situation	General Upgrading	Elite-mass
1. Perception of level of sanctity-expectation for the ordinary person	God expects us to be our brother's keeper. All of us. This is the Christian way of life to have a deep concern for all others. The average man, like all others, has a world-wide apostolate.	God does not expect sanctity of everyone. Most people have all they can do to take care of themselves and their families. They have not the time nor the opportunity to be deeply concerned about others. This latter job is for the chosen few.
2. Perception of the intellectual level of the laity	Most of the people today are becoming more sophisticated intellectually. They are becoming more educated and mentally mature.	Most of the people are simple. We have to talk down to them. We must make things easy or they will not understand. A parish priest's work has little to do with the intellectual life.
3. Perception of the place of intellectual training in the Church	Perceives intellectual training as crucial to the Church.	Perceives intellectual training as dangerous or as peripheral.
4. Perception of intellectual independence	Admires intellectual autonomy.	Takes intellectual heteronomy as a "given and expected."
5. Perception of social relations	In peer terms.	In status terms. Always in terms of higher and lower in the power structure.
6. Perception of the laity as others	A varied group with high and low potential —and this is good. Peers, fellow workers in the vineyard of the Lord.	Sheep: routine cases needing routine services. A threat: getting out of line.
7. Perception of role relations in the Church	The day of the diffuse expertise of the priest is over; where the laity are professionally more competent, they should lead in joint programs. Neither the priest nor the laity at present are experts in the needed leader competencies. This is a time to give and take.	In general the priest should lead, the laity follow, whenever they join in programs. No special competencies are present, but God guides the priest in the leader role.

were expected to emphasize general upgrading over the traditional elite-mass orientation.

Figure 7.1 reports the results of the codings of the "general upgrading" versus "elite-mass" themes. The graphs indicate how many of the ten men in each orientation were coded as having, the "general upgrading" definition of social class.[7] It is amply evident from the graphs that defining role relations in peer terms is consistently characteristic of VC men and, in all cases but one (graph 5), it differentiates them from all the other groups to a significant degree.[8] In every case the INC men represent an extreme position away from the upgrading category. All the graphs represent dichotomies more than continua and, as predicted, distinguish the VC men as peer oriented in their role relations, whereas all the others have a hierarchical orientation. This general upgrading position is an adaptation characteristic and is concerned with changes in traditional role structuring in the division of labor. Power orientation of IC men probably prevents them from being open to this kind of change, whereas VNC men are likely to be deeply attached to the long tradition.[9]

[7] There was a coding for "not ascertainable," but it was used infrequently. Not expressing the characteristic graphed, in most cases, means expressing the alternate characteristic described in the themes. Occasionally, but only where indicated, it means expressing a mixed form. Only those categories are recorded which were reliable and significant. In the scoring procedure, each of the five sections of the interview was read in entirety and coded independently of the other four sections. This was done in such a way that the coding for the previous section could not be seen when succeeding sections were coded. If a man received the same code number three out of the five possible times, he was coded as having that characteristic.

[8] The Fisher Exact Probability Test was used to determine if results could be expected by chance. For an explanation of the Fisher Test see Quinn McNemar, *Psychological Statistics* (New York: John Wiley & Sons, Inc., 1955), pp. 147, 244.

[9] The cultural embeddedness of a way of defining the situation is an important factor in explaining this kind of response that is not recognized in the Adorno *et al.* study of *The Authoritarian Personality*. When, for example, a study using the F test was done in Syria, the high level of authority-oriented responses was better explained by cultural factors than by personality variations. It might very well be that the VNC men are more oriented to a "long tradition" without deep need disposition functioning to preserve this orientation, whereas INC men are more likely to represent the psychologically committed. See E. Terry Prothro and Leon Milikan, "California Public Opinion Scale in an Authoritarian Culture," *Studies in Motivation*, David C. McClelland, ed. (New York: Appleton-Century-Crofts, Inc., 1955), pp. 289-96.

1. High level of sanctity expectation of ordinary person.

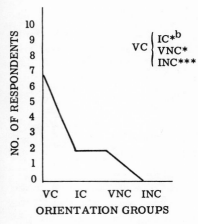

2. Expectation of rising intellectual level of laity.

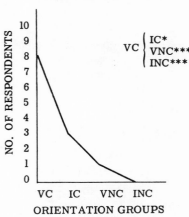

3. Perceives intellectual training as important.

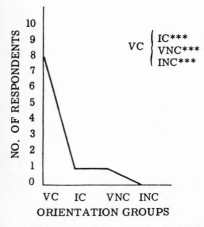

4. Values intellectual autonomy.

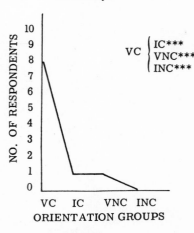

a *Respondents low on the position graphed were high on alternate positions as listed in Table 7.1.*

b *By Fisher Exact Probability Test the probability that these differences are due to chance are: *—beyond .05; **—beyond .01; and ***—beyond .001.*

figure 7.1.

GENERAL UPGRADING THEME (BY ORIENTATION GROUP).

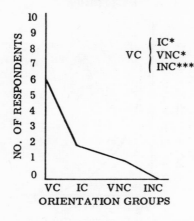

5. Perceives social relations in peer terms, not status terms.

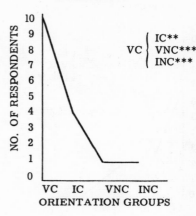

6. Perceives laity as equals rather than subordinates.

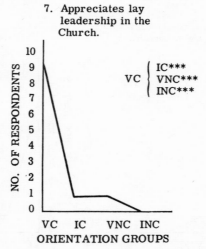

7. Appreciates lay leadership in the Church.

ᵃ *Respondents low on the position graphed were high on alternate positions as listed in Table 7.1.*

ᵇ *By Fisher Exact Probability Test the probability that these differences are due to chance are: *—beyond .05; **—beyond .01; and ***—beyond .001.*

figure 7.1 (continued)

GENERAL UPGRADING THEME (BY ORIENTATION GROUP).

**THEME 2—SOURCES OF SOCIAL REGULARITY,
INTERNALIZED PRINCIPLES OR IMPOSED ORDER**

The categories of the elite-mass and general upgrading type shade into the next set that is concerned more directly with perception of the source of social order. Here the dichotomy occurs between the perception that a shared style of life and belief is the source of social order and the idea that order is imposed by authority figures asking for and getting what they want. Table 7.2 gives the categories for this set.

In this set of themes—perception of social order as derived from "internalized and shared principles," as opposed to the source of order in "imposition of commands"—the VC and VNC groups should be distinct from the two interest groups whose concern is more with power relations either in the command or obedience role. The three categories related to this idea are (1) perception of child training, (2) perception of people's response to authority, and (3) perception of the source of social action in principle or power. Figure 7.2 describes the distribution of scores.

As expected, the two interest groups are high on all three measures, but contrary to expectation, the VNC group is really just as high as the interest groups. This is probably due to the nonchange factor, for what is being measured here is whether an internalized sense of responsibility for bringing one's own behavior into line with one's principles is a better way of understanding the establishment of a stable social order than submission to and respect for commands and expectations of superiors. Old traditions in most cultures, rising as they do from an elite-peasant base, seldom present the idea of the average individual reaching a maturity equated with a capacity to make responsible decisions. The ideal offered for the peasant is the submissive man accepting unquestioningly the guidance of his "betters" and for the noble, *noblesse oblige*. It is really not possible to respect independence in individual behavior unless there is developing evidence of general upgrading through more universal and effective education, practice in self-government, experience in managing one's own affairs, and the like. If a man is still thinking of the average man as necessarily naïve, dependent, self-oriented by nature, he will not be

table 7.2

CONTENT OF INTERNALIZED PRINCIPLES AND IMPOSED ORDER DEFINITIONS OF THE SITUATION

Theme—Source of Social Regularity in Internalized Principles or Imposed Order

Definition of the Situation	*Internalized Principles*	*Imposed Order*
Perception of child training	Perceives child training in terms of growth in capacity to take responsibility, initiate, and create.	Perceives child training solely in terms of obedience and respect for authority.
Perception of how people respond to authority	The expected pattern runs from external control to internal control.	The expected pattern runs from conformity to rebellion.
Perception of source of the impetus to social action	Principle, deep belief in the need of it, prompts social action.	Expediency is usually the source of social action (that is, things are programmed only when the pressures become unbearable).

Power and influence prompt social action (that is, when those in power want action they initiate or get action). |

too enthusiastic about training him to make his own decisions in place of the "safer" training in obedience to the elite. Evidently this value of "responsible choice-making" does not have priority in the traditional repertoire of the VNC oriented man, whereas obedience and respect for authority undoubtedly do. That this is not merely speculation is shown in the following evidence. In response to the question: "In the training of children what do you think is the most important thing they should be taught, considering the times in which we live?" the number who said spontaneously, "obedience and respect for authority," ranged as follows: VC-1, IC-5, VNC-6, INC-8. The other answers included love, responsibility, self-discipline, religion, how to study, and "something different for each child." Evidently the embeddedness of this priority explains the high ranking of the VNC group on this measure.

1. Child-training emphasis:
   Obedience rather than
   responsibility.[a]

2. Response to authority:
   Conformity to rebellion
   rather than internal to
   external control.

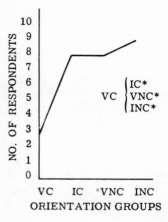

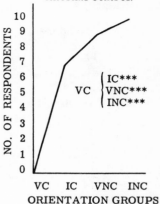

3. Perceives source of
   social action in power
   and expedience not
   principle.

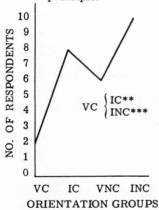

[a] *Respondents low on the position graphed were high on alternate positions as listed in Table 7.2.*

figure 7.2.

SOCIAL ORDER PERCEIVED AS IMPOSED BY COMMANDS
RATHER THAN ESTABLISHED BY COMMITMENT TO SHARED
PRINCIPLES (BY ORIENTATION GROUP).

**THEME 3—PERCEPTION OF SOCIAL ORDER
AS PERMANENT OR CHANGING**

This theme flows right along from concern with principles or power. Table 7.3 gives these categories.

For this third theme—perception of a permanent or changeable social structure—the IC group was expected to be more similar to the VC group than to the other two. As the following two graphs show, this is true to a significant degree for the first category but scarcely so for the others. With an emphasis on power, it may be that IC people perceive change as manipulated by the individual. See Fig. 7.3. The blame-assignment category is the only one that shows a significant difference between both change groups and both nonchange groups. It indicates that a willingness to criticize the social system and to initiate a program in an effort to change it is one of the few areas of shared definition between value- and interest-oriented change men.

table 7.3

CONTENT OF PERMANENT AND CHANGING DEFINITIONS OF THE SITUATION

Theme—Social Order as Permanent or Changing

Definition of the Situation	*System Capable of Change*	*System Change Limited*
Perception of the permanency of social structure	Social structure is an object of social change.	Social structure can be changed or adjusted but only by those in power.
		Social structure is a "given."
Perception of the assignment of blame	On the standards and programs of the system that do not meet the demands of the situation.[a]	On the individuals that fail to live up to the standards and programs of the system.
	Sometimes on one; sometimes on the other.	

[a] *This is a case in which the mixed category was the differentiating one. Too few were coded here to make any real distinction by just using this category alone.*

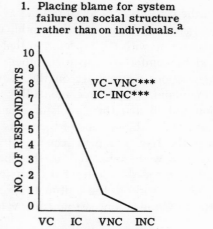

1. Placing blame for system failure on social structure rather than on individuals.[a]

VC-VNC***
IC-INC***

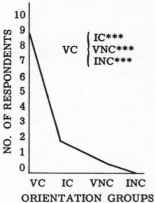

2. Perception of social structure as capable of being changed.

VC {
IC***
VNC***
INC***
}

[a] *Respondents low on the position graphed were high on alternate positions as listed in Table 7.3.*

figure 7.3.

PERCEPTION OF SOCIAL STRUCTURES AS PERMANENT AND HENCE INCAPABLE OF BEING CHANGED BY MAN (BY ORIENTATION GROUP).

THEME 4—OPEN OR CLOSED TO THE WORLD

The categories related to the fourth theme—open or closed perception of group relations—reflect the historical grounding of New England Catholicism in the minority status of Catholics in nineteenth-century America, and the peasant ethnic origins of most of the population. The perception of the Church as catholic, that is, universal, so typically a part of the idea of the Christian message, is constantly confronted with another image of the Church as an exclusive in-group whose main function is to protect its members from the inroads of unorthodox, secular, competing, or hostile out-groups. There are both general and specific forms of this perception of the world as Table 7.4 indicates.

The categories dealing with the perception of social systems as open or closed, whether the other system is the rest of the world, Communism, or any out-group, were set up with the expectation that only the adaptively oriented would be comfortably open to others. The goal-seeking and integration functions concentrate on the in-group, and those concerned with maintaining pattern could still be embedded in the ghetto tradition and all that this entails of alienation for out-groups. Examination of Fig. 7.4 shows none of these sets completely closed to others except the INC group as seen in all three graphs. Only four of the VC men were completely in the open-to-others category. All of the rest were coded as somewhat open (graph 1). On the perception of the secular world as the legitimate object of Church activity (graph 2), the INC men alone see no truth value in

table 7.4

CONTENT OF OPEN AND CLOSED TO THE WORLD DEFINITIONS OF THE SITUATION

Theme—Open or Closed to the World

Definition of the Situation	*Open*	*Closed*
Perception of the secular world	As the logical object of Church activity.	As a passive "given" to which the Church has no commitment.
		As standing hostilely outside the Church.
The self's relation to out-groups	Open.	Closed.
	Somewhat open.	
Perception of Communism	A powerful and competing ideology challenging us to live the Christian commitment.	A powerful and competing ideology requiring power to be used against it.
		A diabolic instrument not to be handled by human means.

1. Self's relation to
   out-groups-open.[a]

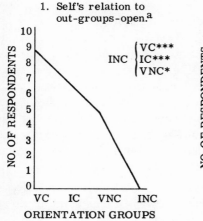

2. Open to world-wide
   apostolate.

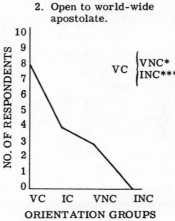

3. Communism, a challenge
   to live a more
   Christian life.

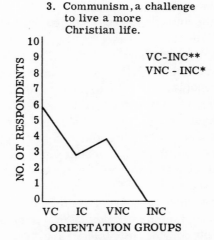

[a] *Respondents low on the position graphed were high on alternate positions as listed in Table 7.4.*

figure 7.4.

OPENNESS TO OTHERS (BY ORIENTATION GROUP).

this idea, and they alone completely reject the idea of treating Communism with charity rather than hostility (graph 3).[10]

Only VC men were expected to be open to the world, and they are not as open as expected. A group without boundaries is a Christian concept, but it can be interpreted in different ways. An "elite-mass" definition makes of the rest of the world "sinners to be saved," and a "general upgrading" definition makes of others "brothers in Christ." Both definitions are quite common. The second one is currently leading to a surge of interest in ecumenism. These categories dealing with perceptions of other groups are closely related to the next set dealing with world views.

THEME 5—WORLD VIEW: COSMOPOLITAN OR LOCAL

There seems to be a striking difference among people in the breadth of vision they bring to a decision-making situation. Some extend their view over the whole world and broad spans of time; others include just the immediate locality in which the decision will actually be effected. This can be characterized generally by Gouldner's terms "locals" and "cosmopolitans."[11] Table 7.5 gives the categories that were used to pick up the differences in world view.

This cosmopolitan or local outlook on the world formed a dichotomy, with the VC group coded eight or ten times in the "cosmopolitan" category and the other three groups coded three or fewer times in this direction, the majority of their codings being "local." This was expected for INC men since "own" group is the expected orientation of all who identify with the system as it is currently organized. It was not expected for the IC men.

The patterns shown in the graphs on Fig. 7.5 are so consistent that each one merely reinforces the others in revealing that the VC men alone are openly viewing their priestly apostolate in terms of all mankind.

[10] This category is coded from very little information that was derived from the last section of the interview schedule. For this reason a man received a score if he exhibited the characteristic even once.

[11] Alvin Gouldner, "Cosmopolitans and Locals: Toward an Analysis of Latent Social Roles—I," *Administrative Science Quarterly*, II (1957), 281-306.

table 7.5

CONTENT OF WORLD VIEW DEFINITIONS OF THE SITUATION

Theme—Cosmopolitan and Local World Views

Definition of the Situation	*Cosmopolitan*	*Local*
Perception of size of the world	Consistently takes a world view.	Consistently takes a parochial view.
	Some local but more generally a world view.	Some world view but more generally local.
Perception of size of the group for which he is responsible	The frame of reference for choice of action or comment about life is the whole world, the human group, the universe, the common good, all God's children.	The frame of reference for choice of action or comment about life is the family, the town, the Catholic community, or some other specific group.
Perception of the object of Church's work	Perceives it as deeply involved in the transformation of the world.	Perceives it only in terms of the local level outside the stream of history and directed to the individual.

THEME 6—THE CHURCH'S RESPONSIBILITY FOR THE WORLD

The last set of categories which could be classified as level of involvement deals specifically with the world of the Church and blends with the one just outlined, which sees the work of the Church in relation to the world. It concentrates more on the need for change in view of the Church's responsibility for the world. Table 7.6 shows categories concerned with the degree of involvement of the priest in the problems the world faces at the present time. These categories, dealing as they do with responsibility for reform, ought to distinguish the value group in every case but the interest group only when conditions are advantageous to the group. As Fig. 7.6 shows, this actually occurs. The VC and IC groups are both dissatisfied with the performance of Catholics in fields of reform at the present time; the IC

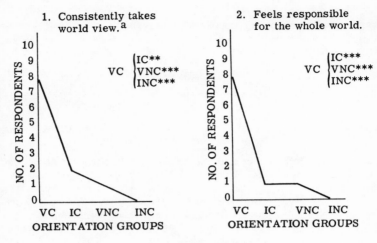

1. Consistently takes world view.[a]

2. Feels responsible for the whole world.

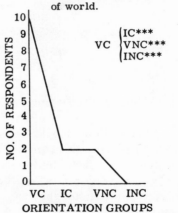

3. Perceives Church involved in transformation of world.

[a] *Respondents low on the position graphed were high on alternate positions as listed in Table 7.5.*

figure 7.5.

COSMOPOLITAN VIEW OF THE WORLD.

group is significantly different from the INC group in relating religion to social issues and being concerned about them. All others are dichotomies. These results suggest that orientation to change is a greater determinant of concern about social issues facing the Church at the present time than is a value orientation. Earlier it was noted that commitment to nonchange tended to shape the views of the VNC men more than did their value orientation.

table 7.6

CONTENT OF RELATION OF CHURCH TO THE WORLD DEFINITIONS OF THE SITUATION

Theme—Church Involvement and Noninvolvement in the World

Definition of the Situation	Involvement	Noninvolvement
Perception of the need of change in the Church in its relation to the world	The Church is an agent of reform for the world; but to perform this role today she must introduce some change.	The Church, as she always operates, is an agent for reform of the world.
		The Church in her mission stands outside the world and its problems and should not get immersed in them at all.
Perception of current performance of Catholics in the work of the Church	We could be doing much more.	We are doing what is expected of us.
		We are doing the best we can to fulfill our Christian duty to the world.
Perception of his own responsibility for the conditions in the world	Feels deeply responsible for the kind of world he lives in.	Feels somewhat responsible.
		Feels no moral responsibility for conditions of the world in which he lives.
Perception of the scope of Christian ethics	Focus on maximal requirements to reach sanctity.	Shifting focus depending on what problem he is analyzing.

table 7.6 (*continued*)

Definition of the Situation	Involvement	Noninvolvement
		Focus on minimal requirements (to stay out of sin).
Perception of priest's responsibility for level of social justice	Social justice is a deep concern.	"Swiss cheese" sense of justice. (Clearly present in some instances, absent in others.)
		No general sense of need for concern for social justice but still some concern.
Perceptions of the relation between religion and social issues	Sees religion bound up with social issues as a norm setter.	Makes a dichotomy between religion and social issues.
Perception of these pressures to change	They are relevant, real, and need attention.	They are not relevant because they are not real.
		If these pressures were real, then attack on them would be relevant, but there is no evidence that they are real.

In summary, the statistical evidence is conclusive that in every category of definitions of the situation the VC set is significantly different from the INC set. There is also some evidence that the IC man is more like the VC man in his willingness to criticize and initiate change in the social structure but that his understanding of social structure is more likely to be in power terms than in terms of internalized principles. There is not sufficient evidence for a distinguishing role of the value orientation in the VNC man. In two instances only do the VNC men move out of the third place in a downward trend away from accepting the value-change oriented stimuli, and in both of these it is a value element that pulls them—treating Communists with charity (Fig. 7.4, graph 3)—and using more value terms than power terms in discussion of social choices (Fig. 7.2).

It can then be concluded that these definitions of the situation are

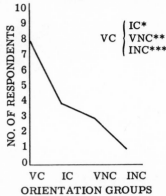

1. Dissatisfaction with current performance of Catholics in field of reform.

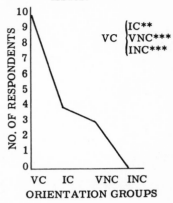

2. Awareness of relation between religion and social issues.

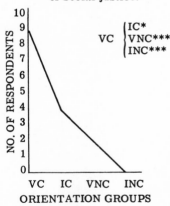

3. Concern for problems of social justice.

ᵃ *Respondents low on the position graphed were high on alternate positions as listed in Table 7.6.*

figure 7.6.

PERCEPTION OF CHURCHMEN AS RESPONSIBLE FOR THE CONDITION OF THE SOCIAL ORDER (BY ORIENTATION GROUP).

4. Perception of the need for change in the Church in its relation to the world.

5. Perception of his own responsibility for the conditions in the world.

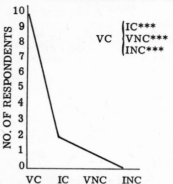

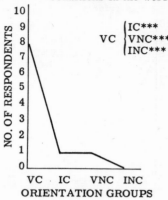

6. Perception of the scope of Christian ethics.

7. Perception of these pressures to change.

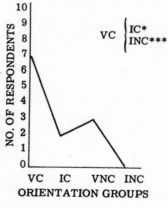

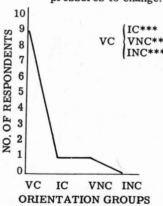

a *Respondents low on the position graphed were high on alternate positions as listed in Table 7.6.*

figure 7.6 (*continued*)

PERCEPTION OF CHURCHMEN AS RESPONSIBLE FOR THE CONDITION OF THE SOCIAL ORDER (BY ORIENTATION GROUP).

related clearly to two of the four orientations, VC and INC, and that the other two orientations always represent some combination of the two extremes. VNC and IC are never distinguishable from each other except in these two cases, when the idea of power draws the IC group and values draw the VNC group. These latter differences are so slight that they have no confirmation here. But there is enough evidence of these differences to urge further refined investigation that focuses more directly on the specific characteristics of the VNC and IC orientations.

Do these findings establish any evidence of a relation between the orientations and the functional categories? Yes; although not a striking confirmation, the following facts indicate some relatedness:

(1) In the first place, the functional problems of adaptation, goal attainment, integration, and pattern maintenance were guides for the selection of the content of these coding categories that discriminated so well in some cases. (2) The orientation of the VC men was overwhelmingly adaptive. (3) An integrative focus was reflected in the INC men perceiving the social structure as given, turning their perceptions to their group rather than toward the world and perceiving the local Church and the local community as the limit of their social responsibility. (4) There was also some slight evidence that IC men were concerned about power, which is a goal attainment characteristic, and VNC men with institutionalized values, which are pattern maintenance factors.

None of these results constitutes clear evidence of the claimed relationship between the orientation groups and the functional problem. To withstand the claims of alternate hypotheses all four categories should respond as predicted. The evidence, however, is substantial that the VC group are adaptation oriented and the INC are concerned with integration functions. Further research is needed on the other two categories.

8

content analysis: styles of response

In a more general way than definitions of the world, styles of response are typical of the different orientation groups. Whatever the content of a communication, the style in which it is couched can communicate resistance or acceptance as well as a whole gamut of other attitudes about the stimulus. The length of speaking time, the logical form, the typical way of interpreting a question or a statement—all can be subtle cues so familiar that they are read and interpreted without analyzing the basis of the interpretation. The question to be explored here is a very specific one: Do the four orientation groups have a tendency to use one style of response more than another? This question is important because if this tendency exists, then the very hearing of a style, by its familiar association, can condition the listener unconsciously or consciously. He can come to expect certain things from the speaker in the way of cooperation, competition, or conflict as well as of more specific processes. In other words, styles of response can be cues always interpreted but seldom analyzed in social relations.

This analysis concentrates not on the special meanings of what was said but on the style in which it was expressed. Did the man hear the question? Did he respond to all of it at once or to a small segment of it at a time? Did he understand the question or ask for clarification, repetition, or rewordings? Did he speak as if these were serious issues in the real world or as if they were hypothetical questions and the experience of the interview just an exercise in logic or opinion exchange? Did he respond with original ideas related to his own specific experience with the issue or in stereotyped clichés applicable to any number of situations in the same way, thus keeping himself at a safe distance from involvement?

Once again the content of the coding categories will be arranged under the general themes that characterize each subset. The themes include: (1) initial response, (2) handling the issue, (3) characteristics of the content of the response, and (4) reactions to the stimuli.[1]

THEME 1—INITIAL RESPONSE

Under initial response the code dealt with the way the respondent indicated that he perceived the issue. Table 8.1 records the differences. In each case acceptance or evasion is operative, but the categories indicate the manner in which this is done.

As Fig. 8.1 shows, these issues were accepted and responded to with understanding only by the VC men.[2] The issues were accepted and responded to with interest by IC men (see graph 1), but not understood by them (graph 2). This is particularly important in view of the fact that most of these statements were drawn from the writings of today's outstanding theologians in the Church, and the IC men, though open to change, were responding to stimuli grounded in values that currently are not richly institutionalized in the local Church community. Finding the questions incomprehensible, claiming, "It does not make sense," and resisting their full meaning were all taken as styles of response, because it was amply evident from the pretesting sessions that for those who accepted these statements with concern

[1] The source of information used for developing these categories for coding styles of response was the bibliography and papers of David McClelland's Harvard seminar in content analysis, Social Relations 243, given in the Spring of 1962. Of special help was Edwin Schneidman's "A Psychological Analysis of Political Thinking: The Kennedy-Nixon Great Debates and the Kennedy-Khrushchev Grim Debates" (unpublished manuscript, Harvard University, 1961).

[2] Only those categories that proved to be reliable and differentiating are reported here. A subjective evaluation is made by the coder and therefore makes the intercoder reliability check an essential requisite for including a category in the analysis. The standard for intercoder reliability was .8; the same coders were used as with the definitions of the situation.

table 8.1

CONTENT OF THE INITIAL RESPONSE CATEGORY

Theme—Initial Response

Style of Response	Accepts the Stimulus	Evades the Stimulus
Area of the issue covered	Responds to the statement as a single stimulus even though he makes divisions in his answers.	Responds to one aspect of the statement but ignores others.
		Does not respond to the statement directly but begins with something irrelevant or indirectly related.
Reaction to the statement or question	Sees the full meaning of the question and responds to it.	Resists the full meaning of the question.
		Claims the question does not make sense.
Acceptance of the problems	Identifies these issues with his own interests.	Shows little concern about the issues.
	Becomes interested in the procession of issues.	Resents all this criticism.

there was no confusion about their meaning.[3] What the results indicate is that when presented with a stimulus not in line with one's preferred way of thinking, it is customary to respond to only a part of it, or to misunderstand it, or to be indifferent or resentful toward it. All these responses block further comprehension to some degree, and this is one way that the barriers to communications are preserved.

THEME 2—HANDLING THE ISSUE

The method of handling the issue reveals an openness to or rejection of its content. Table 8.2 shows the categorical way one can

[3] Because in the content of these codes there is something similar to the agree-disagree analysis reported in Chapter Six, it is well to remember that the second coder for this set was not the same person who did the agree-disagree coding, and there was never any collaboration between them. In fact they never met.

1. Accepts the total
    stimulus rather than
    just part of it.[a]

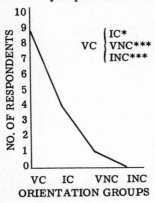

2. Understands
    the question.

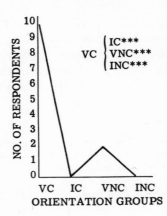

3. Is interested
    rather than resentful
    or indifferent.

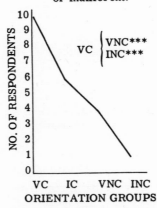

[a] *Respondents low on the position graphed were high on alternate positions as listed in Table 8.1.*

figure 8.1.

INITIAL RESPONSE.

change a situation to a different intent by treating it as unreal or by being inadequately informed.

The first category may need some clarification. It is a common enough tendency when a stimulus to change is proposed to respond as if the questioner were asking, "What would you do *if* something like this should happen (though it probably never will)," rather than "What will you do, since something like this is happening." For example, in response to the question: "In general are you satisfied with

table 8.2

CONTENT OF THE HANDLING OF THE ISSUE CATEGORIES

Theme—Handling the Issue

Style of Response	Issue Is Real	Issue Is Not Real
Reality of the issue	Accepts the issue as real.	Answers as to a hypothetical, or "should" statement—as something that should or should not be so.
		Treats the issue as a criticism with no basis in fact.
		Shifts from one focus to the other, for example, hypothetical to real.
Accuracy of information	Sure of his information and information usually accurate.	Unsure, guessing.
		Sure, but his information is not usually accurate.
Relevance	Speaks to the point.	Speaks irrelevantly.

the training methods used in Catholic schools, parish societies for the young, etc.," one man answered:

I would say "yes." Well, I think the training is sufficient and it's good. If the students and the members of the societies cooperate and respond and react, then certainly the results are as good as we can get.

The question did not ask what *would happen* if a certain set of conditions obtained but rather what *is happening*. The respondent supplied the "if clause" and thus avoided the issue presented to him. Even though he has said the training is good, his "if" sentence implies something else that cannot be probed through this "if" barrier.

The technique of being very sure and yet not accurate with reference to the problem raised can be seen in this next quotation. The question was: "Do you usually associate the rise of Communism with failure of Christians to tend to the problems of social justice in their community?" The answer:

> I think the problem of Communism stems, and you know much better than I do I'm sure, from Descartes. Get rid of the idea of God and what do you have?

It is difficult to draw a man back to the real issue from a deviation spoken with great conviction.

From the graphs of these codes it can be seen that only the INC men treat issues as not real. (See Fig. 8.2, graph 1.) This might possibly be related to the description of these men as needing to preserve the *status quo* for their personal stability, that is, for personality reasons. Such an interpretation seems reasonable if it is correct that these stimuli are in fact impinging on the Church currently in the local community. To treat them as not part of reality, when so much is currently being done concerning them, is to deny reality.

Even though four INC men address the issue, the INC group stands at the bottom of a downward trend in failing to speak to the point (Fig. 8.2, graph 3). Not speaking to the issue is a commonly used device that not only avoids facing the change stimulus in the current situation, but also limits considerably the information that can be shared with a respondent, thus protecting him from developing further information about the stimulus object. He thus immunizes himself from the future recognition of this problem as one he has met before. The initial confrontation is postponed each time. There are respondents who have developed technique for responding to all the issues in this style. This may be one of the most important ways for resisting change.

The most striking difference in style is in reliability of information.

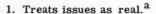

1. Treats issues as real.[a]

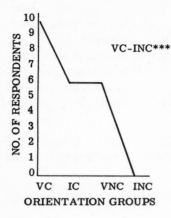

2. Sure of information used and information accurate.

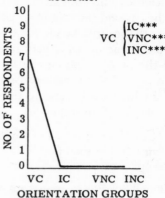

3. Speaks to the point.

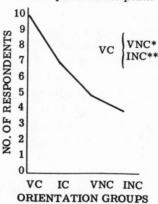

[a] *Respondents low on the position graphed were high on alternate positions as listed in Table 8.2.*

figure 8.2.

HANDLING THE ISSUE.

Evidently reading the "right" literature makes a big difference in knowledge on these topics, since VC men excel here (Fig. 8.2, graph 2), and the census data revealed that VC men alone read consistently the literature from which these stimulus statements were selected. This is an indication of the degree to which choice of reading influences perception of current issues. It still leaves unanswered that important problem of what determines choice of reading. Why do some priests prefer *The Priest, The Homiletic and Pastoral Review,* and *The American Ecclesiastical Review,* which resist these ideas, whereas other priests prefer *Theological Studies, Theology Digest,* and *Catholic Biblical Quarterly* which explore them? Why do the lay-controlled journals, *Jubilee, Cross Currents,* and *Commonweal,* follow the thinking of the second set and reject the first? These questions are raised because they point to a possible answer to the selectivity in the priests' reading. *The Priest* and *The Homiletic and Pastoral Review* are in-group oriented and written for and by priests. They deal with all aspects of a priest's life. They are oriented to the function of integration and they resist innovation. The other journals deal primarily with theology and religion and are written for all interested in these disciplines. They are adaptation oriented. It is important to remember that the census data indicated that level of education was not a distinguishing factor, and that among the younger men there were no other distinguishing sociological characteristics except choice of reading matter and political orientation. This does not mean, however, that reading determines these orientations, because some of these men do not read any of these journals.[4]

THEME 3—CONTENT OF RESPONSE

The two sets of categories that reflect style of content are given in Table 8.3. The issues posed in the interviews were presented as general trends needing to be curbed or general new ways needing to be adopted. When someone limits his consideration of them to a

[4] Thirty-four per cent of the VC men and 12 per cent of the INC men read *Jubilee;* 32 per cent of the VC men and 11 per cent of the INC men read the *Theology Digest* and/or *Theological Studies* and the *Catholic Biblical Quarterly;* only 17 per cent of the VC men and 7 per cent of the INC men read *Cross Currents.*

recitation of single anecdotes, in the frame of "I knew *a* case like that once," or "Here is *an* instance of the very thing you mentioned," followed by a long discussion of a single incident, the device needs examination. It eventually reveals itself as a distractive technique

table 8.3

CONTENT OF RESPONSE CATEGORIES

Theme—Content of Response

Style of Response	*Rich and Relevant*	*Vague and Peripheral*
Generalization	Speaks of the issue as a general problem with specific applications.	Applies the issue to some specific problem ignoring its generality or denying it.
Content	Unusual and enlightening explanations and analyses, generally.	Stereotyped explanations, generally.

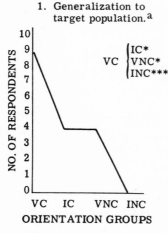

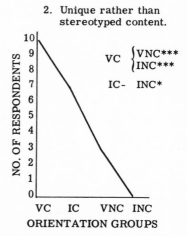

[a] *Respondents low on the position graphed were high on alternate positions as listed in Table 8.3.*

figure 8.3.

CONTENT OF RESPONSE.

deflecting attention from the issue, because after a while the questioner learns that every effort to return to the issue will produce another long anecdote and time is passing.

The table shows that it is predominantly a characteristic of the INC group to fail to generalize to the target population (Fig. 8.3, graph 1), and the codings reveal that they substitute for this the practice of discussing specific cases. Use of unusual and enlightening content rather than stereotyped matter clearly differentiates both change groups from nonchangers (Fig. 8.3, graph 2). This is probably due to the fact that the resistance to these stimuli in the nonchange oriented has to be couched in terms of what is familiar in their socialization process and, because this is now part of the tradition, it has a familiar stereotyped ring.

THEME 4—REACTION TO THE STIMULUS

The three kinds of "reactions to the stimulus" that were coded are given in Table 8.4. It seems that the man whose own security is threatened by change stands out in his total rejection of criticism as a legitimate tool of discussion or exploration of a problem

table 8.4

CONTENT OF THE REACTION TO THE STIMULI CATEGORIES

Theme—Reaction to the Stimulus

Style of Response	Expresses Involvement	Expresses No Involvement
Use of criticism	Criticizes and takes responsibility for the criticisms he makes.	Characteristically defends the Church against criticism.
Suggests solutions	Worked out plans, ideas, and theories he is willing to share.	Presents no solutions.
		Refers to existing solutions which he approves and identifies with.
Action	Is action oriented with respect to these issues.	Is not action oriented with respect to these issues.

when he takes his public position (see Fig. 8.4, graph 1). What follows then is the presentation of an idyllic order of peace, harmony, and tranquility. This statement by one IC respondent in a large city parish of 10,000 is typical. In response to the question, "Do you ever worry about command-obedience relations in the Church today?" he observed:

> I'd answer that by saying that there are different conditions here. We have an excellent class of people with both the school and home training which are conducive to absolute cooperation with the priests and very little difficulty. Of course, problems do arise but they are all solvable. . . . In fact, obedience here today is like daily living; it is a natural flow of cooperation.

From the frame of reference of this priest, this truly describes the condition of his parish as he perceives it, with an established order which he controls and directs with an untiring daily vigilance. From his frame of reference there really is the order of the kind he describes in his parish today. Yet, on the same issue a VC man also located in a large city parish responded:

> Well, of course, there is the criticism that we have to think as we are commanded to think, that our people are priest-ridden, priest- or Bishop-ridden. This won't be good for developing the laity. We have an immature laity now because there has been too much dependence. I have a difficult job in my group to listen to something that comes out in a debate. Somebody wants to know what Father thinks. It really isn't important what I think. I don't think this is good. I think it is better if they are standing on their own feet, doing their own thinking, making their own decisions. That's why I think that this idea that we must obey Father, we must obey the Pastor—there is a certain danger in it.

From Fig. 8.4, graph 2, it can be seen that both interest groups were most reluctant to propose solutions to these value-oriented problems, and from graph 3 that the VC men stand alone in being oriented to action.

ANALYTICAL VALUE OF STYLES OF RESPONSE

Do these findings warrant conclusions about specific relations of certain styles of response to resistance or openness to change? From

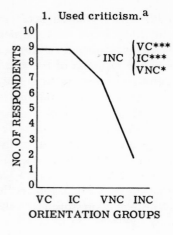

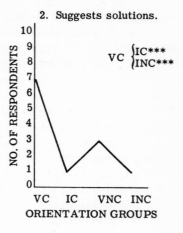

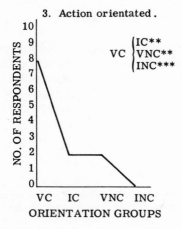

a *Respondents low on the position graphed were high on alternate positions as listed in Table 8.4.*

figure 8.4.

REACTION TO STIMULUS.

the statistical measure of significant differences from chance, there is ample evidence that these men do not come from the same populations with reference to their style of response to these stimuli. Both kinds of change men respond to the whole meaning of the stimulus, but only VC men understand that meaning clearly. So from the very outset there exist barriers to communicating even the stimulus itself. Only VC men have correct information about the stimulus area even though it is richly reported in current literature. This is where knowledge of what the various orientation groups read is so critically important. As the *Voting* study of Berelson demonstrated, men tend to read what reinforces their predispositions to believe.[5]

In summary, these codes suggest that only VC men apparently are anxious to believe in the existence of problems pressuring for change for value-based reasons. Interest-nonchange men stand alone in not recognizing the reality of these issues. This condition is probably due to their high tendency to evade issues that are related to change. They have then no opportunity to learn about them. What VC and IC men say about these issues is relevant and indicative of some thought, since it is characteristically enlightening and unusual. The nonchangers resort to the cliché and the stereotype to explain the existence of problems proposed here. The interest groups both express opinions freely but often unsubstantiated by evidence. All but the INC men feel secure enough to criticize, but only value men are ready with solutions and willingness to turn plans into action. It could be that these styles of response, to the degree that they seal a man off from experiencing stimuli to change at the conscious level, are major factors in resisting change in the historical process.

[5] See Bernard Berelson *et al.*, *Voting, A Study of Opinion Formation in a Presidential Campaign* (Chicago: University of Chicago Press, 1954).

9

content analysis: mechanisms of defense

Complex factors operate in the determination of man's orientation to the world. Personality, situation, history, culture, and social system all contribute directives whether they be in the form of motivation, exemplars, functional necessities, or expediencies. Once a man has defined a given situation, however, and responds to it as defined, he comes to experience congruence or lack of congruence with the definitions and expectations of others. Whenever such experience generates anxieties, he tends to defend his positions consciously or unconsciously in order to protect his image of himself as a reasonable being. Such behavior is defensive and there is rich psychological literature dealing with unconscious motivation to explain it.[1]

The last set of coding categories attempts to determine whether or not characteristic defenses are used by the four orientation groups— VC, IC, VNC, INC. Due to the absence of depth analysis in the interview data there is no claim that this analysis touches deep psychological roots. The question is rather whether or not certain verbal responses that reflect the content of typical defenses are more char-

[1] Defense mechanisms are ways of justifying one's own behavior, ways of thinking or of responding to interpersonal situations so that one does not have to change what he does not want to change. They have two characteristics: (a) they deny, falsify, or distort reality and (b) they operate unconsciously so that a person is not aware of what is taking place. See Calvin Hall, *Theories of Personality* (New York: John Wiley & Sons, Inc., 1957), p. 49.

acteristic of one of the four orientations than of another. If such should prove to be the case, this would be one more piece of evidence that responses to pressures to change are received in characteristic ways that set up barriers to or open the way to initiation of change in currently existing institutionalized behaviors.

ROLE AND STRUCTURE OF DEFENSE MECHANISMS

Since defenses are usually thought of as idiosyncratically related to dynamic personal needs for security, understanding, acceptance, and the like, it is legitimate to ask why defenses should appear at all in a study of this kind. Because childhood experiences like living with poorly educated parents or in a home dominated by father or mother, or the type of school attended, did not show significant correlation with the orientation sets, it was necessary to search for causal relations in more microscopic interpersonal units than identifiable group-types like family, work groups, school and community peer groups. This is where defenses become relevant processes to consider. An examination of what kinds of mechanisms are related to rejection of value-oriented change stimuli should throw some light not only on how changes are responded to, but also on how differently oriented people use the repertoire of defenses. Then the available knowledge about defenses can be related to the findings of this study for further research into the personality factors involved.

Defense mechanisms are methods of resolving interpersonal conflicts when the user, for any reason, fails to handle the existential situation in all its dimensions. The defense is used as a means of reducing the anxiety generated by some conflict between what the actor ideally would like to do and what he actually does. He uses the mechanism to preserve an acceptable concept of himself in the interpersonal situation. The psychoanalytic school's study of unconscious motivation has developed an extensive literature analyzing several different kinds of defenses.[2] The six mechanisms used here were

[2] The idea of defense mechanisms was originally developed by Freud. Specific defenses are defined and analyzed by Anna Freud in *The Ego and Mechanisms of Defense* (New York: International Universities Press, 1946). O. Fenichel develops a classification of defenses in *Psychoanalytic Theory of Neurosis* (New York: W. W. Norton & Company, Inc., 1945). The source directly used for this study is Nancy E. Waxler, "Defense Mechanisms in Interpersonal Behavior" (unpublished doctoral dissertation, Radcliffe College, 1959). The Waxler

chosen because the literature on this topic suggested that these kinds of defenses used to reduce interpersonal anxiety can be coded from written records.[3] The brief descriptions of these six mechanisms given in Table 9.1 will later be reinforced by examples from the interviews.[4]

Even though the function of defenses will probably prove to be one of the most productive factors in the study of the relation of the value, interest, and change orientations to the process of social change, the material to be presented here cannot claim to be more than suggestive for two reasons: (1) there is no depth analysis with which to check the findings; (2) there is no satisfactory reliability check.[5]

HYPOTHESIZED DEFENSE MECHANISMS
BY ORIENTATION GROUP

Using the four functional problems of adaptation, goal attainment, integration, and latent pattern maintenance as guides, the following hypotheses have been developed as to how the four orienta-

---

analysis of defenses, following the lead of Rollo May, *The Meaning of Anxiety* (New York: The Ronald Press Company, 1950), draws from Freud's later works on anxiety and explains it as arising not so much from intrapsychic processes as from interpersonal relations, from the endeavor to relate the self to the environment. The intrapsychic process then becomes significant only as a means of coping with the interpersonal world. Waxler notes that this interpersonal focus is reinforced by the psychoanalytic theories of Karen Horney and Harry Stack Sullivan, who describe defenses using interpersonal concepts. See Waxler, pp. 14-15, and all of Chapter Two, entitled "An Interpersonal Theory of Defense."

[3] In this study, the "other" with whom the subject is interacting is the person whose critical statement is presented for his evaluation and comment. The subject was expected to respond to it as he would have characteristically if the quotation had been presented to him in any unstructured social situation. The mechanisms chosen for this analysis include those that can be coded from written records without making too many assumptions that could be verified only by some form of depth analysis. Other mechanisms including undoing, reaction-formation, displacement, introjection, and identification-with-the-aggressor were not chosen because of the extent to which motivations would have to be read into the written records.

[4] For a more elaborated description of these mechanisms, see Waxler, "An Interpersonal Theory of Defense," pp. 31-42.

[5] A time-cost problem was involved here. Two brief attempts were made to train a student to do this coding, and both results revealed that this is a task for a clinician. Just as the coding for the other categories ran over a hundred hours, the same amount would be necessary here. It seemed better for a first attempt to look for patterns in this study and later to go further with the analysis of defenses when funds are available and the project is demonstrated to be worth the investment.

tion sets should use the defense mechanisms. From the start it was expected that VC men would have much less need of defense when expressing their views on these issues than would the other groups. This was expected because the stimuli were all couched in terms favorable to their previously adopted orientation to values and change. These men do not, however, experience security in the positions they

table 9.1

DEFENSES USED AS CODING CATEGORIES

Name of Defense	Explanation
Denial	The subject fails to see any relation between reality and the stimulus statement.
Rationalization I	The subject may either accept or reject the stimulus but in either case explains it away.
Rationalization II	The subject clearly sees the existence of the criticized condition; not, however, as an evil to be eradicated but rather as a natural element common to all situations in which humans interact. (This may be a definition of the situation rather than a defense.)
Displacement	The subject blames existing conditions on some person or group to which the subject does not belong or, if he does belong, he speaks of them in this case as, "they," thus dissociating himself temporarily from the group.
Regression	Even if aware of the existence of the condition described and the need for the change, the subject leaves all responsible action to others. A typical example: "It's not my responsibility, I'm not in charge," or "I'm not going to stick my neck out," or "Nobody cares what I think."
Isolation	Expressing awareness of a situation at the knowing level without the normally expected evidence of feeling. (This is just one form of isolation known as intellectualization.)
Turning-against-the-self	The subject accepts the criticism with an overwhelming expression of guilt as if he or his group alone were responsible for the existing situation.

hold on these issues when they interact with their fellow priests. This is well documented in the interviews. They frequently perceive themselves as different and are characterized as "radical" by some of their peers. But because their position is currently reinforced by some of the most recognized thinkers in the Church and because their aspirations turn to the needs of the whole world, a concern so in line with their fundamental Christian commitment, it was felt that the interpersonal pressure they receive from their fellow workers would not generate the anxiety that seeks support in defenses. The one mechanism that was postulated for them was a tendency to overblame themselves and the Church with which they identify themselves for perceived inadequacies in existing institutions. This is an adaptive focus. In the same line, then, the INC men should use more denial than anything else, since change is a threat to the current integration of the system. They should also use regression, because in this they seek refuge in the security of childhood integration. They should use displacement on out-groups, since this reinforces identification with the in-group. If the functional hypothesis is correct, the system is itself a struggle for power for IC men, so they will use displacement to reject competition from others and to avoid concern with problems other than those with which they are concerned. For the same reason they will use rationalization I and intellectualization, a kind of isolation that recognizes the need for change but fails to express the feeling expected of one who is involved. Their use of defenses will be centered on rejection of those changes which they perceive as not fostering the group goals in which they are interested. VNC men should have to use much more rationalization, since they are oriented not only to the values that give meaning to the system, but to the *status quo* which in the course of time, through expediency and struggles for power, can come to exploit those very values. INC men will also have to use much rationalization, perhaps more than anyone else, since their functional concern should be to preserve the *status quo* irrespective of any new exigencies that pressure to upset the group structure as it is currently integrated at the normative level and as it is reinforced by the current sanction system. For achieving the goals of the system as well as for preserving its integrity in its present form, the rationalization that claims that "what is, is what ought to be," is a useful device. For this reason both interest groups should use what is here called rationalization II, the equating of what *is* with what *ought to be*. Table 9.2 summarizes the expected pattern of use of defenses.

SUMMARY PROFILE OF DEFENSE MECHANISMS BY ORIENTATION GROUP

The coding of the interviews revealed the distribution of defenses described in Fig. 9.1. The results would be meaningless with-

table 9.2

DEFENSES PREDICTED FOR EACH ORIENTATION SET

Orientation Set	Expected Defenses
Value-change	Turning against the self
Interest-change	Displacement Rationalization II Isolation (Intellectualization)
Value-nonchange	Rationalization I
Interest-nonchange	Denial Rationalizations I and II Displacement Regression

out the additional information from the Mann-Whitney U Test that the differences between groups are significant in some cases. These significances indicate that the differences are not due to excessive use of mechanisms by certain men only.[6] These differences could not be expected to occur by chance and hence suggest that these men in the use of defenses come from different populations.

From the graph of denial (Fig. 9.1) it becomes clear that when

[6] To obtain these probabilities with the Mann-Whitney test each respondent was ranked first on the number of times he used a given defense based on a possible total of fifty-seven times. Fifty-seven equaled the number of stimulus statements and questions in the interview. Each of these was taken as a scoring unit. Within a unit a defense may have been used a number of times but was scored only once.

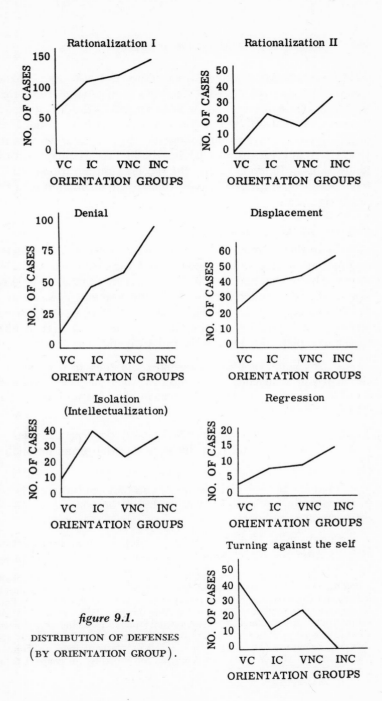

figure 9.1.

DISTRIBUTION OF DEFENSES
(BY ORIENTATION GROUP).

reality is presented in value-change terms, the result is a progressive retreat from this reality, with the INC men farthest from the real, VNC men next distant, and IC men nearest to the VC men who, in this case, are least subject to defense strategy. Ordinary rationalization, displacement, and regression follow the same trend as denial with the INC group in every instance having the highest frequencies. Isolation tends to be an IC defense, and the second kind of rationalization is a tendency of both interest groups, though the distinction is not statistically significant.

USE OF RATIONALIZATION

In the analysis of the interview schedules it was evident that rationalization frequently accompanied other mechanisms, but always the rationalization supplied an answer that made further exploration of the issue unnecessary as far as the respondent was concerned. For instance, in answer to the question: "Do you ever worry about obedience as a problem in the Church?" one man both denied the issue and explained it away in the following manner:

It's not a problem except now and then in a parish where a curate may have difficulty, and I find that when that does occur usually it is because of some psychological element that has nothing to do with organization or canon law.

That was an IC man's way of defining and avoiding an issue.

A VNC man responded to the same question using rationalization II:

It is a problem and will always be a problem because it is the core of the Church. "Whatsoever you bind shall be bound . . . "—that is the question of authority.

Rationalization II is a homemade category to code a particularly characteristic response.[7] Sometimes when a criticism was presented

---

[7] It has been pointed out to me that rationalization II is probably not a defense but rather a definition of the world in which these men define human nature and the world as basically evil and then act in terms of this definition. I think there is a certain validity in this, but because they are all Catholic and claim to accept the Christian ethic, I would prefer to define this definition of what is as what ought to be, as a distortion in terms of the basic values to which they are committed. This very issue is the basis of the current criticisms within the Church of what is being called now a "Sin morality" in contrast to a "love

the respondent would agree that the condition did exist and then add an explanation that this is the way things should be. Usually this was done by explaining it as some law of "nature" or some "inevitable condition" or what would "normally be expected of any man." The following response is another example of this. The stimulus statement begins: "We tend to stand up and play our full role as citizens only when as a group we are in some way being threatened. . . ." The respondent replied, when asked what he thought of this criticism:

> I agree that we tend to stand up and play our full, our full complete role only when there's a group somewhere being threatened. We are not different in that from other elements in the community. They all do.

Perhaps a more striking example of this type of defense is the response to the question which asked: "Do you think it is true that the average Catholic as a result of the training we have given him is more concerned with individual sanctification than with a deep concern for the people of the world?" Fourteen different men answered this with the same general idea found in the following examples.

> Yes, but I think it's part of his human nature. The idea of self-preservation and first of all the sanctification of his own soul.

Another answered:

> Salvation is a terribly personal thing and first of all I must use the means to gain my own salvation; having done that I can branch out and project myself to help others. I cannot have the knowledge to love my neighbors unless I love myself first.

A third said:

> He is concerned with individual sanctification because that is the first obligation. And to say that he is more concerned with his individual

---

morality," which is the basic Christian position. In this regard theologians like Gilleman and Jacques Leclerq and Thils represent the value-change critics, who deplore the "formula moralists"—those who evaluate behavior as permissible not in terms of the ideal of love but in terms of a minimal that is required to keep out of Hell. See James Connolly, *Voices of France*, pp. 156-57; 198-200. See also Gerard Gilleman, *The Primacy of Charity in Moral Theology* (Westminster, Md.: Newman Press, 1949); Gustave Thils, *Théologie des Réalités Terrestres*, 2 vols. (Bruges: Desclée de Brouwer, 1946-1949); and Bernard Häring's, *The Law of Christ, Moral Theology for Priests and Laity*, trans. Edwin C. Kaiser (Westminster, Md.: Newman Press, 1963).

sanctification than he is with the common good is true, and it's a good thing it's true. It's the right thing. I disagree entirely with all these statements.

And a fourth said:

Well of course religion in a way teaches us to be selfish, because we've got to save our own soul first, then save others afterwards, do a good job with our own souls and deal with others afterwards.

All of these men and the other ten who used this rationalization answered an unqualified "no" to a question immediately following which asked: "Is it possible for a Catholic to save his own soul without a deep concern for his neighbor?" Their unqualified "no's" are evidence of the mechanism operating in the initial response. They recognize the second great commandment in this second question, but they have added a dimension about loving themselves first with a primacy in time built in, and this, they claim, is right.

USE OF DENIAL

Recalling the high incidence of evasion recorded for INC men on the agree-disagree scale, and of speaking irrelevantly on the styles of response, and of perceiving these pressures to change as unreal on the definitions of the situation codings, it becomes apparent that INC respondents represent people facing stimuli to change by not facing them at all. This is done by a whole battery of mechanisms in speech and action that keep their world quite free from the inroads of new value-oriented ideas. There is nothing subtle about these denials from the point of view of the hearer. For instance, when asked if he finds any cause for lack of the critical attitude in Catholics in methods used in university teaching, one man replied:

Many parts of this are completely wrong. . . . If you have a good professor and he or she is intelligent and can explain himself clearly, there are very very few occasions when you would want to question them or demand an explanation . . . further explanation . . . as to what they said. They . . . they may say to you, "Well now go out and get reference works and look up further things on the subject," but the basic facts are usually there . . . at least in my experience, I never had professors who were deficient in the presentation of his or her matter. Never.

One statement claimed that Christians have supported programs that benefit them without ever troubling themselves as to whether they violated justice. It was followed by the question: "If you look at conditions today in South Africa, Belgian Congo, South America, and India as well as in our own South and in our city slum areas, do you think this statement has any relevance?" The respondent answered:

That didn't apply to Catholics. It would only apply to some Christians who are not Catholics. . . . That criticism was not deserved by Catholics. [The respondent then listed all the encyclicals that have handled problems of social justice as evidence.]

When asked: "Do you think there is any need for a warning like this: "Churchmen have not pondered enough the case of Galileo?" the respondent answered:

I don't think any case in history has been pondered more deeply and controversially than the case of Galileo. There's a great deal been said about it, and most of the critics of the Church in that matter had no understanding of the position of the Church.

When asked: "Do you think the majority of non-Catholics who oppose the public activity of the Church in the community have this view of the Church [as a power image]?" another man responded:

I think the Protestants, at least the ones I've met, haven't any particular view of the Church at all. [Probe: Why is that?] Probably because they were trained in that direction. As I mentioned before, I think the Protestants are halfway dead. And their image of not only the Church but of God Himself is rather nebulous.

In each of these cases the stimulus statement is simply rejected without any serious exploration of why the statement was made. The respondent never comes to the point of taking the content seriously in any sense.

USE OF DISPLACEMENT

That previous example was not only a denial but also a displacement on a clearly perceived out-group. Sometimes these men attacked the critic who made the stimulus statement. For instance, after hearing Monsignor Ellis' criticism of the Catholic as anti-intellectual one man replied:

> I don't know this Father Ellis here—sometimes it might be attractive, you're stamping yourself as an intellectual—just a bit different and having the courage . . . not the courage, but the daring and the boldness to attack certain ideas of the Catholic Church. You may want publicity, you can get it that way.

What distinguishes displacement from objective criticism is the unreasonable element, the overgeneralization, and the attributing of unworthy motives without evidence. There is a form of this displacement so familiar that it is easy not to notice how successfully it deflects effort. One man used this standard form. He could have been answering any one of the questions. He said:

> Well, it would seem to me that a statement like that would be made by someone that's got an axe to grind or is kicking against the goad for one reason or another. It wouldn't seem to me that a statement like that would be based on a good Catholic foundation.

This is a very primitive way of avoiding the issue, since it leaves no room for further discussion. It calls the case closed.

USE OF REGRESSION

Regressions were not coded often for any in the sample. Those that were noted were mainly attitudes toward authority figures in the form of indirect aggressions against the power others possessed, or escapes from thinking that one has responsibility to act by giving total responsibility for action to a higher status person. It chiefly appeared in comments like this: "It's not my responsibility, I'm not in charge," or in accepting something just because of the status of the speaker in such formulas as, "Well I suppose it must be so if he says it is."

USE OF ISOLATION

Isolation was a much more difficult mechanism to code. It was expressed more by an atmosphere than in words. It usually took the form of a calculated analysis of a problem that normally would generate expression of sympathy, indignation, or action-oriented concern of some form, but which in this case lacked the accompanying affect. The following examples will clarify what was coded. When asked if he thought Catholics were more concerned about their own individual sanctification than about the needs of the people of the world, one IC man replied:

> I'd say, yes. The average Catholic, I think—there are some of course who would be considerate of others—but I think that probably the average Catholic wouldn't. [Probe: Why do you think that?] I don't know, I don't think I could quote you any specific incidents. I don't think I've thought of it that way before.

The comment ended abruptly at this point. He had nothing more to say. It is this cutting off from further expression of concern that marks the response as isolation. He had analyzed a situation to be lacking in what one would expect from a Christian commitment and, despite his priestly role, he goes no further. In the same frame an INC man answered to the question, "Do you ever worry about command-obedience relations in the Church?"

> Well, frankly I don't worry about it because I maintain, as I think every priest should do, to do his duty and don't worry about other things.

This was coded as isolation without sufficient evidence in the words but more from the lack of further comment. Later in the same interview when he was asked: "Do you think young priests have sufficient opportunity to develop and carry out their creative ideas?" he replied:

> No. You can't even move without getting permission. (Laugh) [Probe: And why is this?] It's probably good discipline, but we can't write an article or even publish a bulletin on a weekly basis without first getting permission from the Chancery office. And they want to know what you're going to do, how you're going to do it, and by the time you get around to answering their questions and so forth and so on, give them a brochure on what you're going to do, you get so disgusted you say, "Oh, forget it. . . ." We do have some crackpots in the clergy, and I'm probably one of them (laugh); but still at the same time a great deal of initiative is being stifled by regulation.

This second response, so full of deep feeling and concern, almost bitter, reveals the function of the mechanism of the earlier reply. A kind of stoic acceptance has become this priest's reaction to an area in which he is very sensitive. This stoicism gives way to earnest outburst when the problem is pressingly important to him.

In the next example denial and isolation combine in a response to the question: "Do you think young priests have sufficient opportunity to develop and carry out their own creative ideas?" (This man is a pastor.)

> No, and they never will. (Laugh) [Probe: Why not?] They go off on tangents. (Laugh) They all come back to the same thing after a while. They all come back.

Taken by themselves these mechanisms would give a rather gloomy picture of an existing social system, unless one remembers that these responses are not distributed indiscriminately nor are they used frequently by many. They are defenses to resist change and to preserve a definition of the situation that, unless probed, can prevent any upsetting urgency from reaching the spiritual sensitivities of these men. They are important to examine because they are not used at random, and they demonstrate that mechanisms can be used by people at all levels of education and dedication when they are pressured to move in directions which they resist.

USE OF TURNING-AGAINST-THE-SELF

These defenses stand in striking contrast to the responses of others presented with the same stimuli but who were committed to values grounded in their Christian beliefs and open to change in institutionalized ways of doing things. Value-change men used some mechanisms but with much lower frequency. There was one way of responding, typical of this group, however, that could be classified as the defense called turning-against-the-self. As a defense this is a tendency to overblame the self for the existence of a given condition. Actually the stimulus statements themselves were statements of self-blame made by people in the Church who recognized that despite the divine mission of the Church, a series of institutionalized patterns were today inhibiting its fundamental purpose. It may be that only those who shoulder blame for a situation can initiate change in the situation. If this is the case, then turning-against-the-self becomes a mechanism for change.

Statements were coded as turning-against-the-self if the respondent actually blamed himself or if he accepted a share of the blame for conditions in the Church by using the pronoun "we" rather than "they" in his statements of criticism. An example of both kinds follows: One VC man, in responding to the question: "How do you explain to yourself that Hitler's regime actually killed six million Jews?" said:

> Perhaps if I knew more about the situation I could say, but in this case it's a woeful lack of charity to be uninterested in the slaughter of six million people. (Pause) I haven't been interested in it, Sister. I haven't bothered to read about it. (Long Pause) To that extent I haven't been Christian. I haven't been my brother's keeper.

Father was so absorbed in this that he did not hear the next question. There is conflict here, and it may be that a long interview, just on this, would have brought it to the surface, but this short statement and the tone in which it was said suggested that this indifference, this confused indifference, would probably continue. Most of what has been coded as turning-against-the-self has a much more action-oriented flavor indicating that the user is identifying himself with a cause or a need to which he intends to attach sufficient affect to energize himself to action, or has already done so. Examples of this run through entire interviews in phrases like these: "Yes, we as Catholics have tended to keep to ourselves, still nursing the hurts of an earlier era. We cannot do this today. We have the work of the Church to do," or "Our schools have fostered a dependency. We have misinterpreted the meaning of obedience in our training. We must share our work with the laity not only in Church finance but in the teaching and liturgical work of the Church."

This tendency to say "we" when admitting to failures in the way things have been done in the past in the Church is a value trait rather than an interest one. This capacity for self-blame seems to be totally lacking in the INC group. This may mean that only those who can identify themselves with blame can initiate reform, though many others at various stages of the reform's progress can participate in it. Maybe only VC men can support the initial program when the risks are high, the possibility of failure great, and the rewards nonexistent as far as anything external to the dedication itself is concerned. Only further study can test these speculations.

TEST CASE: NEGRO HOUSING

In a study of this nature, though the questions are directly related to the happenings of our times, one can still wonder what these men would do if faced with an immediate decision that required action right now, action that would test their orientation to values, interests, and change. Do the same factors operate in such a situation? To explore this problem, an issue was needed that is so currently alive and pressing that a response to it would have to include evidence of how one had handled or was handling the situation. Integrated housing for Negroes proved to be the best such issue. This was a burning problem in the Boston area. This question was formulated to get the respondent's orientation to action and was placed right after he had expressed his opinion as to whether aspirations to sanctity required one today to be concerned about the housing, employment, and education of one's neighbor. It read:

If you were called on by a civic committee to join in a Fair Housing Practice effort to get a Negro family placed in a good home in your parish, a home that they could afford but because of restrictive convenants have not been able to purchase through real estate agents, what would you do?

This is a very direct question, and it is difficult to avoid it. The responses were so strikingly in line with the expectations developed for each of the orientation groups (except the VNC men) that they stand as a confirmation of the whole analysis. Figure 9.2 shows that eight VC men agreed immediately that they would join the committee. One said he would help the family but did not mention the committee. One admitted that he had already refused to join such a committee because he felt it represented special interests and instead went around individually to speak to his parishioners and put an announcement in the parish bulletin urging an open welcome for Negroes. Ten of these

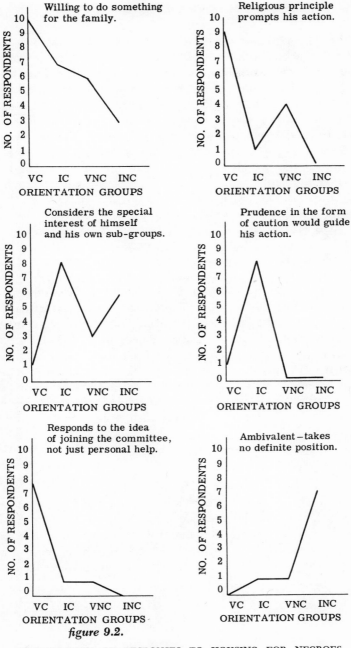

figure 9.2.

DISTRIBUTION OF RESPONSES TO HOUSING FOR NEGROES
QUESTION (BY ORIENTATION GROUP).

men would help in some way. Seven IC men said they would do something, but only one even mentioned the committee. This is that type of agreeing that changes the meaning before responding. They would, after taking precautions to check the credentials of the applying family, handle the situation themselves individually. To most of the IC men this question had no meaning or legitimacy unless it referred to a single good Negro family with an immediate pressing problem.

There was no pattern in the VNC group except that like the interest groups, they avoided the question of the committee and only considered the problem of an individual Negro family needing a home. Only one VNC man used the "prudence" response so characteristic of the IC men. Two answered monosyllabically that they would "Do what they could," as did three of the INC men.

The IC group and the INC group each had a characteristic response, the first a prudential caution, the second an ambivalence about taking any position on the issue at all.

The responses to this question run the gamut of styles of response, definitions of the situation, ways of agreeing and disagreeing that have been discussed in the last three chapters. They constitute a primary source of evidence that men in the same roles do not define the world the same way, do not respond to change the same way, nor do they do so idiosyncratically. The responses vary much more in style between sets, than they do within sets. There is a regularity in the type of response within each set that strongly suggests the existence of a determinant in the four orientations with respect to this stimulus question.[8]

INTERVIEW EVALUATIONS

A final piece of evidence for internal consistency within each orientation set will be found in this last example of the general reaction of each group to the interview experience. It should be recalled that each of these stimulus statements was selected because it represented a pressure to change institutionalized patterns of interpersonal behavior that have become characteristic of some elements in the

[8] For complete records of each response see my "Values and Interests in Social Change" (unpublished doctoral dissertation, Harvard University, June 1963).

Church through centuries. All but one of the stimuli statements were taken from published works of well-known Catholics looking at the Church since World War II. At the very end of the interview this question was posed: "In general, how do you feel about the problems that I have raised today? Do they have any relevance for your work?" The responses to this question were strikingly different for each group. They ranged from a value-change man saying:

Yes. I think they are very significant questions and it's a pity that a lot of them are so late in being asked and even now so late in being listened to by the people who count.

to an interest-nonchange man saying:

Did you raise any problems? I don't know, but I don't think you raised any problems. If there were any that you did raise I don't think there were any serious ones.

Some of the striking contrasts in responses are described in Fig. 9.3. Nine unqualified "yes's" characterize the VC group. The IC men had no unqualified "yes's," and the most common response was that some of the problems were relevant and important and others were not. This is an example of that selective factor that seems to be characteristic of the IC position and that can mean that they respond only to those issues that have special relevance for their own group. The VNC group, as always, is split two ways: five accept the stimuli as important and relevant and five do not. Evasion, the most characteristic response of the INC group, again is the dominant response here, with "no's" in second place. That ambivalence, that incapacity to face the issue, emerges now as the characteristic INC response.

What then can be said in general about the relation between the use of defenses, the functional problems of social systems, and the orientations to values, interests, and change? Nothing can be said conclusively because of the absence of a reliability check, but a summary of the general tendencies is suggestive for further research:
(1) Self-blame and self-criticism seem to be an adaptive mechanism. Dissatisfaction with what is institutionalized is not sufficient to generate that investment of energy necessary to initiate change and to bear the burden of rejection inflicted on those differently oriented to the

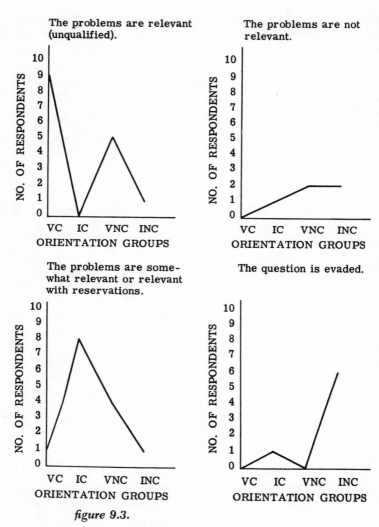

figure 9.3.

EVALUATION OF THE PROBLEMS POSED IN THE INTERVIEW
(BY ORIENTATION GROUP).

existing social system. One must also be able to share the responsibility for existing inadequacies at a feeling level. Thus turning-against-the-self becomes predominantly a value-change mechanism.

(2) Intellectualization and rationalization II (which claims that what is, is what ought to be) seem to be used to keep the system manipulable by those already in power. The isolation of feeling from facts in the intellectualization apparently enables the IC man to be aware of need for change and still invest his energy to change only selectively in terms of those problems that will be of advantage to special interests.

(3) For the INC man to invest his energy in the *status quo* and to reinforce its norms at the affective level, the whole gamut of mechanisms seems to come into play, with denial and rationalization being the major means of controlling anxiety.

(4) It is harder to describe from the evidence in this study what is going on in the VNC group. It is even at times difficult to see a pattern at all, except that these men constantly take a religious point of view, and speak in value terms but also defend special interests, as they cling to the *status quo*. Their mechanisms are mixed. Their agreements and disagreements are unpredictable. Evidently there is a real conflict between preserving meanings and upholding the *status quo* which at times expresses distortions of these meanings.

Finally, when faced with a real stimulus to change that pressures right now, each of these groups calls into play a whole battery of responses and, as predicted, uses them to resist or to accept the stimulus in stylized ways, which is probably in itself a significant mechanism for determining the direction of the social process.

10

conclusion and prognosis

Because broad theories of social change like Marxian conflict theory and Parsonian functional analysis of structural differentiation do not in their present formulations bring the analysis of the change process down to the role level where the decision making takes place, there is no clear way of testing the claims of these theories in the on-going historical process. With current theories in their present undifferentiated forms, it is impossible to examine all the intervening variables between gross interest and value factors and the actual direction history takes. In contrast to these sociological oversimplifications, the existential situation suggests that values and interests operate in quite stylized ways in social relations, sometimes fulfilling the expectations of a Marxian model, sometimes of a Parsonian. This study of Boston priests and their responses to stimuli to change currently institutionalized behaviors was initiated to find out if analysis of patterned responses to historically grounded stimuli would shed any light on how values and interests operate in the wider context of more general history.

PROGNOSIS FOR THE DIOCESE

The findings, which allow for conclusions applicable specifically to the Boston situation, suggest a prognosis. The evidence shows that, in 1961, 35 per cent of the diocesan clergy were VC oriented,

11 per cent IC, 21 per cent VNC, and 28 per cent INC. Although in general VC men tend to be younger, the top scorers in this category are older. Thus, with the trends of the Vatican Council toward change and reform, the over-all picture for the diocese optimistically indicates that Boston priests will cooperate with and initiate these new programs for reform in the Church not because of special interest factors for institutional aggrandizement, but for realization of the basic values of a Christian commitment. Other factors, however, suggest some modification of this optimism. An examination of the high scorers in each of the four categories (see Table 5.2) indicates that value-change men tend to be placed in staff positions that limit them to consultant roles and to decision making in highly specialized areas not in the direct line of command to the diocesan parish system and to the general programming of Church affairs. The pastors of the local churches tend to be predominantly INC men. This split in the division of labor suggests that the diocese can at the same time be articulate in its value commitments to change and resistant in its day-to-day programming of the routine of the parish. At the parish level there still prevails the conception of the social structure of the Church as an unchanging given, of the laity as the masses to be led, and of the apostolate limited to parish boundaries and not inclusive of the world and the larger community. At this level, too, pressures to change are responded to by evasions, and new issues are often handled only at the theoretical level. Here denials and isolations raise barriers to communication and discourage the articulate VC person from surmounting the obstacle of the projection which can place him on the side of the devil and the rationalization which explains his cause away. The strain is greater if, at the same time, the social welfare services, the communication media, and the apostolate to the world at large are in the hands of those for whom the world is their apostolate and the laity their peers.

Those who recognize intellectual autonomy and who regard institutionalized evil as a target for action are ready for reform in the community, the government, the school, the business world, the civil services, and the Church. They are currently open to consider with great seriousness the problems defined by the late Pope John XXIII and by Cardinal Bea, the secretary to the Commission on Christian Unity, as those most pressingly the work of the Church in the world today, namely world peace prepared for through disarmament, aid to underdeveloped nations to handle the problems of poverty, and minority-group problems. All of these problems, if they are to be faced effectively, require restructuring of current patterns institutionalized in local church-community relations. If the staff of the Church is coming to perceive the great relevancy of these issues for communicating the Christian message in our times, and the line of authority is still absorbed in a fatalism that focuses on solutions of human suffering only at the transcendent level or as service to the indigent, then the near future for the Church in Boston will be one of painful misunderstanding as line and staff pull in different directions to achieve similar ends, namely the salvation of the world. But the evidence from the data here is hopeful for the realization of these value-based changes. The number of VC men is increasing among the younger priests and is still substantial among older priests. For the immediate future the critical factor, then, in administration is appointment of pastors and teachers. This is something that can be programmed though age is still the major determinant of appointment of pastors. For the long future the critical factor is the seminary staff and the seminary curriculum. What is being taught and how it is being communicated will set directions for deep-seated identifications that come with the focusing of the enthusiastic dedication of youth on the critical issues for programming action for the fulfillment of the two great commandments. This study in its analysis of the problems pressing the Church in the present century indicates the need of sociological and psychological training for those whose work lies in the sphere of religious teaching, not that these be substitutes for a new and dynamic theology and philosophy but that they enable the religious specialists to distinguish the social, political, and psychological functions of religion from the spiritual, lest that which is end be confused with that which is means, and the unconscious in man or the power structure in the community or economy come to make of the Church a tool for secular ends rather than the means of bringing the secular to its highest realization in the ultimate good.

Beyond these specific conclusions applicable to Boston and perhaps generalizable at least as hypotheses for a number of other Church situations currently pressured to change, the results suggest that the same model can be used to examine the change process in political, educational, business, and other social systems by simply redoing the value and interest items in content relevant to the system under examination.

METHODOLOGICAL IMPLICATIONS OF THE FINDINGS

Even beyond these empirical applications, what is the relevance of the study for a theory of social change? Four findings contribute to a method of predicting the direction of social change: (1) The clearest here is the centrality of the definition of the situation as a determinant of the frame within which decisions are made. Since clusters of actors in the same situation hold different perceptions of the same social world and how it is structured, and act according to how they perceive that structure, information on this dimension becomes a necessary tool for analysis and prediction of change. If some men perceive people as the masses and the elite, while others just as clearly perceive the same people as their peers currently expressing a variety of potential, then knowledge of the roles of those differently oriented is essential for understanding what is going on. Through the instruments used in this study it is possible in any given situation to determine by content analysis just what the views of the world of the actors are and how they influence the choices being made in terms of resisting and accepting change. Orientations to the world act as central conditioners of choice-making. This means that actors in decision-making role relations do not in fact come to share the meanings of problems in their setting before they make decisions about disposing of them, and this is a most common and extensive difference in any given situation. Besides being common it is determinable by content analysis of the dialogue in the change-pressuring process. (2) The second finding is that the very style with which one responds to a stimulus to change is, in itself, a mechanism for conditioning the initiator to continue to press or to retract or deflect his efforts because of the positive or negative sanctions he receives in the form of defenses, evasions, and rationalizations, and this, too, can be measured. (3) A third finding indicates that the very phrasings of agree-disagree responses sets the decision making off in several different directions in terms of whether all, some, or none of the original stimuli is responded to.

Less specifically but quite emphatically the findings demonstrate that a deeply grounded personality factor in the form of the value, interest, change, and nonchange orientations is a major determinant of the way people play their social roles and that these orientations are predictably related to the responses of the actors to historically grounded stimuli. This finding says that the VC, IC, VNC, and INC orientations are intervening variables that can be measured and from which predictions of the direction of future change can be made since response to stimuli to change are patterned in terms of these orientations.

One of the richest theoretical questions that the study presents— what is the causal factor generating these change and nonchange oriented personality types that show a preference for making choices in value or interest terms—is not clearly answered, though direction for further study is clearly suggested. The persistence over time of the orientation types measured by the first instrument and tested by the second some two to six months later led to the investigation of the relevant socialization variables that could have generated these orientations. The significant findings, however, were limited to the fact that VC and INC types are more likely to come from central cities, and VNC and IC types from smaller towns and more in-group areas of the city; that religious liberalism is associated with political liberalism and that reading habits strongly reflect value or interest positions. The hypothesis that the four orientation types are related to the four functional categories of the Parsonian model for the analysis of functional problems of social systems (adaptation, goal attainment, integration, and pattern maintenance), receives much reinforcement from the findings but no clear demonstration of a significant relationship. To test this further, interest-oriented stimuli pressuring the IC and VNC sets will probably be the critical areas for seeking other significant differences.

THEORETICAL RELEVANCE OF THE FINDINGS

At the very general level of the function of values and interests in the process of social change in Parsonian and Marxian sociology, this study proposes modification in the value over interest or interest over value assumptions in the direction of a situationally specific factor. It proposes that a liberal or conservative orientation to change, as well as a particularistic or universalistic orientation to decision making of the actual role players in a given historical moment, are demonstrably determinants of the decision-making process of a magnitude deserving examination in their own right rather than being absorbed into some category of historical trend. Whether or not these category types are peculiar to this moment of history and hence an accident rather than a causal factor is still somewhat an open question. This analysis suggests that when given decision makers are pressured with stimuli to change, their responses constitute typical patterns of rejection or acceptance. These in turn stimulate a limited set of reactions to being rejected, ridiculed, threatened on the one hand, or of being encouraged on the other. A great many different kinds of pressures receive similar kinds of responses because the interpersonal messages are similar and hence arouse similar experiences of pain or pleasure. An avoidance or approach syndrome is generated by the style of response, defenses used, and definitions given to the situation. The latter communicate to the one pressuring for change the degree of openness or nonopenness of the respondent and how much teaching, convincing, or socialization must precede any further attempts to press for change on this particular person. Depending upon the centrality of his position, this can hold up or limit the implementation of new ideas and plans.

It may well be that value-change men are heard with pleasure when they give new definitions to situations needing explanation, not action, but are resisted in stylized ways as described here when action is called for and the decision maker's interests are not served by the proposed changes (when the decision maker is interest-oriented). It may also be that this withdrawal of encouragement along with a distaste for direct interpersonal conflict frequently causes the VC man to move aside from direct action when conflict of interest groups becomes central in a decision-needing situation. Thus the VC men withdraw when the interest-oriented approach. These latter, more oriented to power than to values and more concerned with immediate solutions than with long-range direction, are less inhibited by the fear of open conflict and are now more free to make decisions directed by competing special interests. When, therefore, teaching precedes the value-based pressures, value-directed change moves forward with little stress, since it is reinforced by the approval of those sharing the same principles. But when the situation is unfamiliar and resistance from interest groups rises, the VC men move out, leaving the field clear for conflicting interest groups. The VC men may need some kind of psychic support to continue to pressure when conflict of interests are expressed openly. The presence or lack of this support from some source may be a critical factor in determining their continuing role in pressuring for value-oriented change. This, of course, is a speculation needing further testing.

In conclusion the study demonstrates a value and interest orientation of decision makers as an important variable in determining response to pressures to change, and this in turn suggests that these responses are critically determining factors in setting the direction change will take. More studies will be needed in the fields of politics and business to see if the model developed here for the clergy in the community has the same meaning in other interpersonal systems.

appendix

appendix table 1

VALUE, INTEREST, CHANGE, AND NONCHANGE SCORES OF HIGH- AND LOW-RANKING
RESPONDENTS IN EACH OF THE FOUR ORIENTATION GROUPS

VC		IC		VNC		INC	
					Non-		Non-
Value	Change	Interest	Change	Value	change	Interest	change
V C	V C	I C	I C	V NC	V NC	I NC	I NC
85 - 84	85 - 84	35 - 14	20 - 35	42 - 3	27 - 44	39 - 21	15 - 39
58 - 63	58 - 63	24 - 16	4 - 29	38 - 2	10 - 35	33 - 8	4 - 39
50 - 50	37 - 56	22 - 7	17 - 23	38 - 2	8 - 34	29 - 6	23 - 38
44 - 49	50 - 50	20 - 35	13 - 20	34 - 1	26 - 32	26 - 18	22 - 38
43 - 41	44 - 49	19 - 1	1 - 18	30 - 9	3 - 28	24 - 3	16 - 36
41 - 38	30 - 47	18 - 2	24 - 16	28 - 3	14 - 26	23 - 38	2 - 35
37 - 56	35 - 46	17 - 23	3 - 14	27 - 44	2 - 25	23 - 1	8 - 32
36 - 3	24 - 44	17 - 4	35 - 14	26 - 32	10 - 24	22 - 38	17 - 32
35 - 46	16 - 42	16 - 6	13 - 12	25 - 7	9 - 23	21 - 35	15 - 31
32 - 15	43 - 41	13 - 20	4 - 11	24 - 3	1 - 22	21 - 4	8 - 29
31 - 35	41 - 38	13 - 16	3 - 10	22 - 8	25 - 21	20 - 20	12 - 27
31 - 13	31 - 35	13 - 12	2 - 8	18 - 14	12 - 21	20 - 7	12 - 26

Low-ranking respondents

VC		IC		VNC		INC	
					Non-		Non-
Value	Change	Interest	Change	Value	change	Interest	change
V C	V C	I C	I C	V NC	V NC	I NC	I NC
1 - 13	20 - 1	1 - 18	19 - 1	1 - 2	5 - 1	1 - 1	1 - 1
1 - 13	11 - 2	2 - 8	18 - 2	1 - 5	8 - 1	1 - 5	8 - 1
1 - 13	24 - 2	2 - 8	13 - 3	1 - 6	8 - 1	1 - 17	13 - 1
1 - 15	3 - 3	2 - 9	7 - 4	1 - 22	17 - 1	1 - 25	16 - 1
2 - 15	4 - 3	3 - 10	13 - 4	2 - 7	1 - 2	2 - 9	7 - 2
2 - 20	6 - 3	3 - 14	17 - 4	2 - 10	11 - 2	2 - 14	10 - 2
3 - 3	17 - 3	4 - 5	4 - 5	2 - 25	14 - 2	2 - 22	16 - 2
4 - 3	24 - 3	4 - 29	8 - 5	3 - 5	16 - 2	3 - 4	6 - 3
4 - 9	30 - 3	4 - 11	8 - 6	3 - 7	38 - 2	4 - 7	14 - 3
4 - 10	42 - 3	7 - 4	12 - 6	3 - 9	38 - 2	4 - 12	24 - 3
4 - 11	11 - 4	8 - 8	16 - 6	3 - 28	6 - 3	4 - 12	3 - 4
4 - 29	9 - 4	8 - 5	22 - 7	4 - 16	15 - 3	4 - 12	12 - 4

Mean for entire sample on each variable

Value-change	Interest-change	Value-nonchange	Interest-nonchange
Value—17.81	Interest—11.32	Value—12.96	Interest—12.16
Change—17.56	Change—10.35	Nonchange—11.23	Nonchange—15.30
N = 91	N = 28 .	N = 55	N = 73

ITEM STATISTICS FOR EACH ORIENTATION: INTEREST, VALUE, CHANGE, NONCHANGE; UPPER AND LOWER QUARTILE MEANS BY ORIENTATION SETS; DISCRIMINATORY POWER, STANDARD DEVIATIONS, MEANS FOR TOTAL SAMPLE, MEANS FOR UPPER AND LOWER QUARTILE FOR EACH ITEM UNRANKED BY THE FOUR ORIENTATIONS

N = 259

Interest Scale

No.	Scores Scaled on Interest		D.P.	S.D.	Mean for Total Sample	Mean for Upper and Lower Quartiles of Item Scores Unranked by Sets	
	U.Q. Means	L.Q. Means				L.Q.	U.Q.
1.	5.39	3.05	2.34	2.15	4.50	1.48	6.67
2.	4.03	2.52	1.51	1.91	3.28	1.44	6.08
3.	6.08	3.84	2.24	1.76	5.04	2.19	6.59
4.	5.73	3.59	2.14	1.80	4.56	1.97	6.28
5.	5.67	3.47	2.20	1.77	4.58	2.06	6.34
6.	6.20	4.09	2.11	1.87	5.22	2.34	7.00
7.	6.11	4.61	1.50	1.63	5.55	3.27	7.00
8.	3.78	2.20	1.58	1.90	3.03	1.23	5.96
9.	4.49	2.00	2.49	1.82	3.10	1.20	5.73
10.	5.71	3.38	2.33	1.84	4.68	2.11	6.57
11.	5.26	2.63	2.63	1.97	3.88	1.56	6.35
12.	5.56	3.24	2.32	1.82	4.54	1.98	6.35
13.	5.18	2.66	2.52	1.92	3.76	1.66	6.36
14.	5.52	3.69	1.83	1.74	4.80	2.25	6.50
15.	4.87	2.44	2.43	1.95	3.70	1.50	6.31
Total	5.55	3.16	2.39		4.29	1.88	6.41

Value Scale

No.	U.Q. Means	L.Q. Means	D.P.	S.D.	Mean for Total Sample	L.Q.	U.Q.
16.	6.18	5.93	.25	1.17	6.14	4.75	7.00
17.	4.58	3.21	1.37	2.04	3.61	1.45	6.34
18.	5.72	2.69	3.03	1.83	2.97	1.78	6.30
19.	5.89	4.26	1.63	1.62	5.29	2.91	6.84
20.	4.90	2.76	2.14	2.00	3.76	1.52	6.38
21.	5.96	5.16	.80	2.04	4.45	1.77	6.73
22.	5.01	2.67	2.34	1.93	3.77	1.58	6.26
23.	5.43	2.96	2.47	1.78	4.34	1.97	6.45
24.	5.49	3.21	2.28	1.97	4.34	1.61	6.45
25.	5.50	4.47	1.03	1.69	5.00	2.38	6.66
26.	6.04	4.62	1.42	1.66	5.34	2.75	7.00
27.	6.50	4.53	1.97	1.58	5.54	3.14	7.00
28.	6.10	3.07	3.03	1.99	4.73	1.89	6.75
29.	4.72	1.40	3.32	1.92	3.53	1.47	6.19
30.	6.00	3.27	2.73	1.85	4.67	1.98	6.50
Total	5.60	3.61	1.99		4.56	2.20	6.59

table 2 (*continued*)

N = 259

Change Scale

No.	Scores Scaled on Interest U.Q. Means	L.Q. Means	D.P.	S.D.	Mean for Total Sample	Mean for Upper and Lower Quartiles of Item Scores Unranked by Sets L.Q.	U.Q.
31.	5.13	3.00	2.13	1.94	4.14	1.69	6.42
32.	5.80	3.78	2.02	1.67	4.98	2.41	6.56
33.	5.67	3.75	1.92	1.82	4.89	2.13	6.78
34.	5.60	3.30	2.30	1.87	4.79	1.98	6.58
35.	5.76	4.15	1.61	1.81	5.03	2.20	6.80
36.	5.19	3.06	2.13	1.86	4.26	1.75	6.38
37.	5.44	2.66	2.78	1.90	4.07	1.72	6.48
38.	5.24	3.03	2.21	1.92	4.08	1.64	6.38
39.	5.95	3.73	2.22	1.72	4.95	2.30	6.56
40.	5.15	2.75	2.40	1.78	3.70	1.70	6.08
41.	5.35	3.33	2.02	2.10	4.33	1.33	6.50
42.	5.93	3.92	2.01	1.57	5.03	2.59	6.53
43.	5.96	5.12	.84	1.44	5.54	3.53	7.00
44.	5.83	3.95	1.88	1.71	4.94	2.33	6.70
45.	5.61	3.41	2.20	1.82	4.59	2.13	6.55
Mean	5.57	3.53	2.04		4.62	2.10	6.55

Nonchange Scale

No.	U.Q. Means	L.Q. Means	D.P.	S.D.	Mean for Total Sample	L.Q.	U.Q.
46.	5.92	3.86	2.06	1.65	5.22	2.73	6.73
47.	6.18	3.98	2.30	1.69	5.25	2.56	6.84
48.	5.03	2.07	2.96	1.96	3.61	1.45	6.36
49.	6.12	3.90	2.22	1.65	5.12	2.52	6.72
50.	6.01	3.00	3.01	2.26	4.47	1.31	7.00
51.	5.98	3.33	2.65	1.74	4.88	2.25	6.59
52.	5.04	2.60	2.44	1.84	3.66	1.50	6.03
53.	5.24	2.80	2.44	2.07	3.95	1.50	6.50
54.	5.70	3.67	2.03	1.58	4.96	2.45	6.36
55.	6.14	4.03	2.11	1.65	5.26	2.58	6.83
56.	3.55	2.55	1.00	1.65	3.24	1.64	5.64
57.	6.57	5.55	1.02	1.13	6.22	4.89	7.00
58.	5.36	3.35	2.01	2.00	4.37	1.77	6.63
59.	5.35	3.09	2.26	1.90	4.22	1.72	6.34
60.	5.78	3.41	2.37	1.83	4.71	2.09	6.61
Mean	5.60	3.41	2.19		4.60	2.20	6.54

COMMUNITY STUDY*

Form C

Subject number _____   Date _____

Directions:

On the following pages you will find a series of statements expressing
opinions of the kind you might hear from persons around you. For each statement
there are a set of six possible answers.

    ∤1 Agree slightly   -1 Disagree slightly
    ∤2 Agree   -2 Disagree
    ∤3 Agree strongly   -3 Disagree strongly

You are asked to read each statement and then write a plus one (∤1) if you agree
slightly; plus two (∤2) if you just agree; or a plus three (∤3) if you agree
strongly; a minus one (-1) if you disagree slightly; a minus two (-2) if you disagree, or a minus three (-3) if you disagree strongly.

    Each statement stresses an emphasis, not an absolute. You are simply asked
to state the direction you would prefer that emphasis to take. If you should have
some doubt or reservation about any of the items, the directions at the top of the
next page suggest what you can do.

    This is not a test of ability. There are no answers that will be scored
right or wrong. Each person's opinion may differ from that of others in many respects. Just answer according to your preferences.

    Be sure to answer every question in some way. This questionnaire is for
research purposes only. Your results will be kept strictly confidential.

    *This is an exact copy of the instrument as it was used in the original study.
    This copy however is coded to show how the answers are to be scored. The
    code appears in the answer boxes: I-Interest item, V-Value item; C-Change
    item; NC-Nonchange item. The three items coded in reverse are indicated in
    the scoring boxes.

COPY OF QUESTIONNAIRE USED TO DETERMINE ORIENTATION
SCORES.

Agree slightly +1   Disagree slightly -1
Agree   +2   Disagree   -2
Agree strongly +3   Disagree strongly -3

Kindly place the numbers with the plus or minus sign in the columns to
the right of each item. Where you are hesitant or uncertain, place a line
(like a minus sign) to the far left of the page beside the item (see
example below) and still take the choice that comes nearest to your opinion.
Any comments you wish to make on the opposite page will be gratefully received. Please mark item numbers beside such comments.

Sample item and sample responses:

The government does not really care what people like me think.	-2
____ I expect the world to be much better off ten years from now.	+3

Start here:

1. The best way to improve world conditions is for each man to take care of his own corner of the vineyard.	1	I
2. If I were to follow my deep convictions, I would devote much time to reform movements. This seems to me to be a primary need today.	2	C
3. The society of tomorrow is already developing from the values believed in by people today.	3	V
4. Although change is necessary and can be a good thing, loyalty to the long tradition is the stable base on which we should place primary focus of social concern.	4	NC
5. When I am working at my own job, I get so absorbed in it that I tend to neglect what is going on in the rest of the world.	5	I
6. There is really something refreshing about enthusiasm for change.	6	C
7. Having ideals is a wonderful thing, but realistically speaking, in most of the really important decisions in life, personal or group interests, and not ideals, play the major decisive role.	7	V (Score in Reverse)
8. Young people sometimes get rebellious ideas, but as they grow up they ought to get over them and settle down.	8	NC
9. In times of crisis, it is only natural for men to think of themselves first even though they may be ashamed of it afterwards.	9	I
10. Although the Church is the vehicle of God's grace to man, still it contains at present many social institutions which ought to be changed.	10	C
11. When I think of social reform, I think of things I believe in so deeply I could dedicate all my efforts to them.	11	V
12. By continuing its traditional approach to its teaching role, the Church will better accomplish its mission than by experimenting with new methods.	12	NC

13. Man is not an idealist by nature. It is hard for him not to be motivated primarily by self-interest.
13   I

14. Every great step forward in world history has been accomplished through the inspiration of reformers and creative men.
14   C

15. I have a clear set of values that I hope some day to see implemented in my community.
15   V

16. If I were to follow my deepest concern, I would concentrate on trying to preserve the very best of the long tradition. This seems to me to be a primary need today.
16   NC

17. The ideal of temporal peace inherent in the idea of the state is never strong enough to overcome the dynamic forces of human self-will.
17   I

18. Man should try to rectify in creation everything he can rectify.
18   C

19. Concerns about caution have little place when the issue is one of social injustice.
19   V

20. The future is in God's hands. I will await what He sends and accept what comes as His will for me.
20   NC

21. We have to exercise caution when we act in the local community because it is so easy for those outside the Church to misinterpret what we are trying to do.
21   I

22. The main function of the intellectual is to meet the unknown and unstructured future creatively.
22   C

23. Because I have not given it a great deal of thought, I would find it quite difficult to say right now what I think ideally the world ought to be like.
23   V (Score in Reverse)

24. In the final analysis the strongest basis for planning for the future is to trust to the experience of the past and base the decision-making on the facts, the historical facts.
24   NC

25. When people are better, the world will be better. Let each man then tend to his own reform.
25   I

26. The current situation in the Church calls for change. We must respond at once.
26   C

27. I am so deeply concerned about social injustice that I would rather join a community program that is endeavoring to eliminate it and take a chance that the program will be good than miss an opportunity to do something about it.
27   V

28. I like conservatism because it represents a stand to preserve our glorious heritage.
28   NC

29. If you have dedicated yourself to the work of some group or organization, it is only right that you should put the interests of that group before those of all other groups.
29   I

30. If you want to get anywhere, it's the policy of the system as a whole that needs to be changed, not just the behavior of isolated individuals.

30   C

31. When I hear of people who are deprived of freedom and of just treatment I really get involved; I find myself planning how I can help them.

31   V

32. From my experience, I have learned to believe that there is nothing new under the sun.

32   NC

33. When you come right down to it, it's human nature never to do anything without an eye to one's own profit.

33   I

34. Any organizational structure becomes a deadening weight in time and needs to be revitalized.

34   C

35. The most important issues in the world today are issues of social justice.

35   V

36. In general, it seems to me that though reformers come and go, still the world goes on in the same pattern of ups and downs.

36   NC

37. When you are young you can afford to be an enthusiast for reform, but as you grow older you learn that it is the better part of wisdom to confine your efforts within your own field.

37   I

38. Liberalism is a good thing because it represents a spirit of reform. It is an optimistic outlook expecting meaningful advance. It may not always represent justice, light, and wisdom, but it always tries to.

38   C

39. Man is neither egoistic nor altruistic by nature, but he has a tremendous responsibility to become the latter.

39   V

40. An organizational structure that has stood the test of time is a far better instrument for carrying out programs today than one that is just emerging from the experimental laboratory.

40   NC

41. In the last analysis, it's having the power that makes the difference.

41   I

42. The Church in her teaching must adapt to the findings of science and modern exigencies.

42   C

43. The things I think are important and valuable for the good life are so clear to me that I could list them right now with little difficulty.

43   V

44. The main function of the intellectual is to evaluate critically all that is past.

44   NC

45. It is really concern for security, personal satisfaction, recognition, and affection which motivate most men in their daily behavior. Ideas about justice and freedom are quite remote.

45   I

46. Re-evaluation and reform are constantly necessary, and I am ever eager for each new effort to make a better world.

46   C

47. An injustice in the local community should never find the Church a silent witness.

47   V

171

48.	Looking back over the long history of the Church, we have every reason to be proud of the contributions she has made in the societies where her influence has penetrated.	48	NC
49.	No matter how wonderful the ideas you are trying to get across may be, you cannot do a thing unless you have the powers that be on your side.	49	I
50.	The world as it is is a pretty good place. We really don't need all this concern about change.	50	C (Score in Reverse)
51.	A priest can hardly call himself a shepherd if he is not as deeply involved in the social welfare of people as he is in giving spiritual service to his parishioners.	51	V
52.	My first reaction when I think of the future is to be aware of its dangers.	52	NC
53.	Because it is often difficult to know what values are involved in social action programs, I prefer to wait to see which way things are going before joining them.	53	I
54.	I am not satisfied with the world as it is, and I spend now, and intend to spend, much more of my life trying to change it.	54	C
55.	I would rather be called an idealist than a practical man.	55	V
56.	Rather than get upset about them, we have to learn to live with most of the conditions in the world as they are.	56	NC
57.	No matter how good a cause sounds, and no matter how moral the principle on which it is based, still an administrator should follow a wait-and-see policy so he will not get involved in any embarrassing situations from which he will have difficulty withdrawing afterward.	57	I
58.	Would that the middle-aged and elder citizen could retain that enthusiasm for initiating change that frequently characterizes the rebellious youth.	58	C
59.	When I am dealing with the problems of my own job, I find myself constantly trying to make decisions that will help solve the bigger issues of justice, etc., for all mankind. The world's problems are very much my problems.	59	V
60.	Not change, but permanency and stability are what we are aiming for in the work of the Church.	60	NC

172

selected references

The books suggested here are but a few among many that throw light on three main areas of the research: (1) the place given values and interests in theories of social change; (2) the problems of change pressuring the Catholic Church at the present time; (3) the function of attitudes in personality and social structure. They are suggested as leads to new works appearing in all three fields.

Robert N. Bellah, *Tokagawa Religion* (New York: Free Press of Glencoe, 1958), demonstrates how a Parsonian model can be used to reveal the process of modernization in Japan. In this study values are treated as grounded in religion and functioning as legitimators of changes leading to the rapid industrialization of Japan. It is an application of Weber's thesis developed in *The Protestant Ethic and the Spirit of Capitalism*, translated by Talcott Parsons (London: George Allen & Unwin, 1930), and it proposes that religions internalized in personality systems set the style of behavior and the motivation that leads to an acceleration or depression of the process of industrialization. Neil Smelser, in *Social Change in the Industrial Revolution* (Chicago: University of Chicago Press, 1959), applies a theory of social change to the industrial revolution with values again playing the dominant role and interests sparking subservient action. Wilbert E. Moore's *Social Change* (Foundations of Sociology Series, Englewood Cliffs, N.J.: Prentice-Hall, Inc., 1963) summarizes and organizes theories of the primacy-of-value type. Two studies that clearly take exception to the primacy of value as a determinant of social change and see interests of power groups as the basic determinant of historical direction with values subservient are Ralf Dahrendorf's *Class and Class Conflict in Industrial Society* (Stanford, Cal.: Stanford University Press, 1959) and Barrington Moore's *Political Power and Social Theory* (Cambridge, Mass.: Harvard University Press, 1959). All four books use history for case material. For a study that treats religion as the ground of values and then as an initiating factor in social change as well as a source of preservation of the *status quo*, see Christopher Dawson, *Religion and Culture* (New York: Sheed & Ward, 1938).

The following books trace the problem of pressure to change in the Catholic Church. The number of books available at present is so great that any selection becomes somewhat arbitrary. William Ferree's *The Act of Social Justice* (Dayton, O.: Marianist Publications, 1951) is a reprint of a doctoral dissertation done at Catholic University in the early 1940's which demonstrates the problem of structured evil and the necessity of planned action for the reform of the social system. It explains why the emphasis on social justice has only recently developed in the Church. Thomas O'Dea's *The American Catholic Dilemma* (New York: Sheed & Ward, 1958) is a sociological analysis of conflict in a modern industrial society with its changing role expectations for clergy and laity. Gustave Weigel, S.J., *Faith and Understanding in America* (New York: The Macmillan Company, 1959), develops the thesis that the formally organized Church is not a strong influence in major decision making today and then suggests how this can be changed. Robert D. Cross, *The Emergence of Liberal Catholicism in America* (Cambridge, Mass.: Harvard University Press, 1958), sets the stage for the problems deriving from the historical development of the Church in this country. Emmanuel Cardinal Suhard's *Growth or Decline: The Church Today* (South Bend, Ind.: Fides Publishers, 1948) is a book which examines the problem of current social responsibility of the Church. Jean Daniélou's *The Christian Today*, translated by Kathryn Sullivan (New York: Desclee, 1960) elaborates the themes suggested by Cardinal Suhard and spells out the mission of the Church in the modern world. Yves Congar, O.P., *Lay People in the Church*, translated by D. Attwater (Westminster, Md.: Newman Press, 1957), reconsiders the role of work in the world and the value and importance of the laity. Difficult in translation, it is nonetheless a landmark in the new emphasis on the place of the laity in the Church. Daniel Callahan, *The Mind of the Catholic Layman* (New York: Charles Scribner's Sons, 1963), is a good example of pressure from within the Church for some basic changes in social structure and organization in order that laity can work in the Church on programs suggested by biblical, liturgical, and ecumenical themes and move into the world with the social doctrine of the gospels. Albert Dondeyne, *Contemporary European Thought and Christian Faith*, translated by Ernan McMullin and John Burnheim (Pittsburgh, Pa.: Duquesne University Press, 1958), explains the challenge of modern philosophies like existentialism and logical positivism to traditional thinking in the Church. W. K. Grossouw, *Spirituality of the New Testament*, translated by Martin W. Schoenberg (St. Louis, Mo.: B. Herder Book Company, 1961), demonstrates the social import of the gospels for our times. Hans Küng, *The Council, Reform and Reunion* (New York: Sheed & Ward, 1962), handles the command-obedience problem, social responsibility, respect for the intellectual life—all in line with the possibilities of a reunited Church for our times. Abbé Michonneau, *Revolution in a City Parish* (Westminster, Md.: Newman Press, 1949), explains how problems of motivational awareness and dependency training can be solved by changing the patterns of interpersonal relations in the parish. Hans Urs von Balthasar, *Christianity and Science* (Westminster, Md.: Newman Press, 1958), works out at a deep intellectual level how the problems of the anthropologist affect the thinking of churchmen. Gordon Zahn, *German Catholics and Hitler's Wars* (New York: Sheed & Ward, 1962), is a carefully documented sociological study of the effect of dependency training on response to a serious moral crisis.

The following articles are but a few of the many incisive analyses of the problems of change facing the Church at the present time. They have been selected in view of the five areas treated in this study: Karl Rahner, S.J., "Reflections on Obedience," *Cross Currents*, X, No. 4 (1960), 362-74; Michael Novak, "The Priest in the Modern World," *Review for Religious*, XX (July, 1961), 265-71; M. D. Chenu, O.P., "Toward a Theology of Work," *Cross Currents*, VII, No. 1 (1957), 175-87; Gustave Weigel, S.J., "American Catholic Intellectualism: A Theologian's Reflections," *Review of Politics*, XIX (July, 1957), 275-308; Ernan McMullin, "Science and the Catholic Tradition," *America* (December 12, 1959), 346-50; Servais Pinckaers, "Revival of Moral Theology," *Cross Currents*, VII, No. 1 (1957), 56-66; M. D. Chenu and Friedrich Heer, "Is the Modern World Atheist?" *Cross Currents*, XI, No. 1 (1961), 5-24; François Mauriac, "Traditionalists and Innovators: Foes within the Church?" *Cross Currents*, XII, No. 1 (1962), 1-12; and Marc Oraison, "The Psychoanalyst and the Confessor," *Cross Currents*, VIII, No. 4 (1958), 346-76. Two encyclical letters published by Pope John XXIII focus the entire attention of the Church on the problems of social responsibility: *Mater et Magistra* [English title, *Christianity and Social Progress*] (New York: The America Press, 1961); *Pacem in Terris* [English title, *Peace on Earth*] (New York: The America Press, 1963).

Four works dealing with the psychological problems of attitude and attitude formation that form a part of the value-interest/change-nonchange continua include the two psychological studies of T. W. Adorno, *et al.*, *The Authoritarian Personality* (New York: Harper & Row, Publishers, 1950) and Milton Rokeach, *The Open and Closed Mind* (New York: Basic Books, 1960.) Both of these books associate certain views of the world and related attitudes with specific life experiences, especially during the socialization process. The following two sociological studies show the effect of attitude sets on the very structure of social systems: Leon Bramson, *The Political Context of Sociology* (Princeton, N.J.: Princeton University Press, 1961) and Winston White, *Beyond Conformity* (New York: Free Press of Glencoe, 1961).

index

Acceptance-rejection scale in interview evaluation, 95-100 (*table*)

The Act of Social Justice, William Ferree, 29-30, 31

Adaptation as functional problem, 11-12, 18, 139

Adorno, T. W., *et al.*, *The Authoritarian Personality*, 38, 47, 89

Agree-disagree continuum, 92, 98 (*table*)

"America," 68

American Catholic Dilemma, Thomas O'Dea, 57

American Catholic Education Association, 41

"The American Ecclesiastical Review," 131

American Protective Association, 56

Aquinas, St. Thomas, 24, 30

Aristotle, 30

Assent and dissent patterns, 92-95 (*table*) (*fig.*)
  significance of, 95-96

Assimilation, of national groups, 55

Augustine, St., *City of God*

The Authoritarian Personality, T. W. Adorno, *et al.*, 38, 47, 89

Bales, Robert F., 47

Baltimore, Maryland, 54

Bauer, Raymond, Alex Inkeles, and Clyde Kluckhohn, *How the Soviet System Works*, 47

Bea, Augustin Cardinal, 159

Berelson, Bernard, *et al.*, *Voting, A Study of Opinion Formation in a Presidential Campaign*, 136

Bosler, Father, 89

Boston, Archdiocese of:
  assimilation of national groups, 55
  education of study respondents, 63
  family and childhood of study respondents, 61-63
  immigrant groups, 54-57
  Irish in, 55-56

Boston, Archdiocese of (*Cont.*)
  prognosis for, 158-161
  reading habits of study respondents, 64-65
  role in Catholic Church in America, 54-57
  as sample source for study, 44
  social correlates of orientation types, 65-70 (*tables*)
  status of study respondents, 64-65

Carroll, Bishop, 57

"Catholic Biblical Quarterly," 68, 70, 131

Catholic Church:
  and areas of pressures to change, 19, 20, 36-43, 44-45
  clergy-laity relations, 28-29, 31
  command-obedience relations, 19, 20, 36-43, 44-45
  cultural base of pressures to change, 33 (*table*)
  ecumenical concern, 26
  in France, 31
  independence training for children, 19, 20, 36-43, 44-45
  individual perfection, 27-28
  Ireland, Archbishop, 19
  motivational awareness, 19, 20, 36-43, 44-45
  in New England (see Boston, Archdiocese of)
  in nineteenth century, 19
  as object for functional analysis, 19
  and Protestant Reformation, 24-25, 26
  respect for intellectual life, 19, 20, 36-43, 44-45
  response to strain areas, 20
  responsibility for the world, 117-123 (*tables*) (*figs.*)
  as sacramental system, 25-26
  and social justice, 29-31
  social responsibility, 19, 20, 36-43, 44-45

177